BLOOM'S

ReViews

COMPREHENSIVE RESEARCH & STUDY GUIDES

Ernest Hemingway's

The Old Man and the Sea

Edited & with
an Introduction
by Harold Bloom

Printed and bound in the United States of America.

3 5 7 9 8 6 4 2

Library of Congress Cataloging-In-Publication Data

Ernest Hemingway's The old man and the sea / edited and with an introduction by Harold Bloom.
p. cm. -- (Bloom's Reviews)
Includes biographical references and index.
Summary: Includes a brief biography of the author, thematic and structural analysis of the work, critical views, and an index of themes and ideas.
ISBN: 0-7910-4071-2 (hc)
0-7910-4144-1
1. Hemingway, Ernest, 1899-1961. Old man and the sea. [1. Hemingway, Ernest, 1899-1961. Old man and the sea. 2. American literature—History and criticism.] I. Bloom, Harold. II. Series.
PS3515.E37052 1995
823'.912—dc20
95-43498
CIP
AC

Chelsea House Publishers
1974 Sproul Road, Suite 400
P.O. Box 914
Broomall, PA 19008-0914

Contents

Editor's Note 4
Introduction 5
Biography of Ernest Hemingway 8
Thematic and Structural Analysis 11
List of Characters 22
Critical Views
- Ernest Hemingway: The Style of the Novel 24
- Seymour Krim: The Unoriginality of the Novel 24
- Mark Schorer: The Novel as a Fable 26
- Carlos Baker: Santiago's Christ-Like Nature 28
- Clinton S. Burhans Jr.: Santiago as a Tragic Hero 30
- Edwin M. Moseley: The Personal Nature of Tragedy 33
- William J. Handy: Success and Failure in the Novel 35
- Robert W. Lewis Jr.: Santiago's Solitude and Faith 38
- Bickford Sylvester: Symbolism in the Novel 41
- Sheldon Norman Grebstein: The Structure of the Novel 43
- Joseph M. Flora: Practical Christianity in the Novel 46
- Linda W. Wagner: Hemingway's Language 48
- Jogendra Kaushal: Hemingway's Concept of the Artist 51
- Charles Taylor: Hemingway and Nietzsche 54
- Martin Swan: Women in the Novel 56
- Angel Capellán: Santiago's Spanish Background 58
- Gerry Brenner: Fable and Fantasy in the Novel 61
- James Mellard: Hemingway and Homer 63
- Thomas Hermann: Hemingway and Cézanne 66

Works by Ernest Hemingway 69
Works about Ernest Hemingway and *The Old Man and the Sea* 71
Index of Themes and Ideas 75

Editor's Note

My Introduction rather sadly judges *The Old Man and the Sea* to be an involuntary self-parody. Extracts begin with Hemingway's praise of his own prose, which is countered by Seymour Krim's agreement as to the prose but negative conclusion that the novelist has said it all before. Mark Schorer admires the strength of the fable, while Carlos Baker finds an image of Christ in old Santiago, and Clinton Burhans sees the fisherman as an authentic tragic hero, as does Edwin Moseley.

Inner triumph is stressed by W. J. Handy, as by Robert W. Lewis, after which Bickford Sylvester uncovers the short novel's concluding symbolism. S. N. Grebstein praises the book's structure, while Joseph Flora finds in it "the essence of Christian discipleship."

The sparseness of the prose is analyzed by Linda W. Wagner, after which Jogendra Kaushal adumbrates Hemingway's vision of the artist. Refreshingly, Charles Taylor invokes Nietzsche rather than Christ as the presiding genius of the story. Hemingway's disdain for women is remarked by Martin Swan, while Angel Capellán sets forth the novel's background in Spanish culture.

Mythic fantasy is suggested as appropriate genre by Gerry Brenner, after which James Mellard risks a comparison of Homer and Hemingway. Cézanne is invoked as analogue by Thomas Hermann, who usefully reminds us how formalistic a work *The Old Man and the Sea* is.

Introduction

HAROLD BLOOM

In a celebrated interview with George Plimpton, Hemingway emphasized his art of omission in the short novel whose protagonist he had so deeply identified with himself:

> *The Old Man and the Sea* could have been over a thousand pages long and had every character in the village in it and all the processes of the way they made their living, were born, educated, bore children, etc. That is done excellently and well by other writers. In writing you are limited by what has already been done satisfactorily. So I have tried to learn to do something else. First I have tried to eliminate everything unnecessary to conveying experience to the reader so that after he or she has read something it will become a part of his or her experience and seem actually to have happened. This is very hard to do and I've worked at it very hard.
>
> Anyway, to skip how it is done, I had unbelievable luck this time and could convey the experience completely and have it be one that no one had ever conveyed. The luck was that I had a good man and a good boy and lately writers have forgotten there still are such things. Then the ocean is worth writing about just as man is. So I was lucky there. I've seen the marlin mate and know about that. So I leave that out. I've seen a school (or pod) of more than fifty sperm whales in that same stretch of water and once harpooned one nearly sixty feet in length and lost him. So I left that out. But the knowledge is what makes the underwater part of the iceberg.

The style of Hemingway's remarks is very much the style of *The Old Man and the Sea,* and could be called, rather unkindly, involuntary self-parody. Despite the boast that the book could have been a thousand pages long, the principal fault of what is really a rather long fish story is that it should be shorter. A lyrical storyteller, almost a prose poet, Hemingway risks too many verbal repetitions in *The Old Man and the Sea,* perhaps wrongly believing that they would work as refrains. Santiago the fisherman is rather too clearly Hemingway himself, only fifty-two but romanticizing that he is very much older. The book's allegory is transparent; the writer is at work trying to land the really big book, even though we need not identify the sharks as literary critics (though such a naming would not be altogether inaccurate). We are given a Cuban fisherman who flies a sail that looks like "the flag of permanent defeat." Yet he himself is indomitable: "Everything about him was old except his eyes and they were the same color as the sea and were cheerful and undefeated." The boy who venerates him, a substitute son, associates him with "the great DiMaggio," a linkage that Hemingway is glad to accept for himself. Incongruously, Santiago dreams of Hemingwayesque lions on the beach, and the dreams stimulate the old fisherman's mystical confidence in his craft. Santiago's greatest affinity is with the enormous eighteen-foot fish that he lands, after an apocalyptic struggle, only to lose the fish to the rapacious sharks. It is a unique fisherman who thinks in Hemingwayese:

> Only I have no luck any more. But who knows? Maybe today. Every day is a new day. It is better to be lucky. But I would rather be exact. Then when luck comes you are ready.

That would be persuasive only if Santiago were a sort of John O' Hara or Nelson Algren of a Cuban fisherman, a disciple who has read his Hemingway. The old man, like the boy, and even the big fish, remains so abstract that his heroic ordeal is emptied of much of its pathos. "Now is the time to think of only one thing. That which I was born for." Clearly, to compose the great work: "Now we are joined together and have been since noon."

Though the old fisherman has been compared to Melville's Captain Ahab, harpooning Moby-Dick, the comparison is absurd, and not just because Ahab hates the White Whale while Santiago loves the big fish. We are back in *Death in the Afternoon* as the fish turns into a Spanish bull and Santiago into an intrepid matador:

> The old man dropped the line and put his foot on it and lifted the harpoon as high as he could and drove it down with all his strength, and more strength he had just summoned, into the fish's side just behind the great chest fin that rose high in the air to the altitude of the man's chest. He felt the iron go in and he leaned on it and drove it further and then pushed all his weight after it.

> Then the fish came alive, with his death in him and rose high out of the water showing all his great length and width and all his power and his beauty. He seemed to hang in the air above the old man in the skiff. Then he fell into the water with a crash that sent spray over the old man and over all of the skiff.

What partly redeems Hemingway's allegory is not the old man but rather the sea: "he knew no man was ever alone on the sea." Something of Melville's and Whitman's power of invoking the sea remains alive in Hemingway's book. The sea may be the mirror of a Narcissus, but it surges with life in Hemingway's prose, and we are left wondering how he might have wanted us to allegorize it. ✣

Biography of Ernest Hemingway

Ernest Hemingway was born on July 21, 1899, to Dr. Clarence and Mrs. Grace Hall Hemingway in Oak Park, Illinois. Clarence Hemingway, an avid hunter and fisherman, shared his love of the outdoors with his son each summer at Walloon Lake in northern Michigan, which influenced many of his stories. During the rest of the year, Hemingway attended public school in Oak Park, where he actively participated in athletics and wrote columns in the style of sportswriter Ring Lardner for the school newspaper.

When he graduated from high school in 1917, he skipped college to pursue journalism. For seven months, Hemingway received a valuable on-the-job education as a cub reporter at the Kansas City *Star* but longed to join the American troops overseas fighting World War I. Rejected by the army because of an eye injury, he became an ambulance driver for the Red Cross. In July 1918, he was seriously injured by shrapnel near Fossalta di Piave, Italy, and was decorated by the Italians for his bravery. After recuperating in Milan, he returned to Michigan in January 1919.

Bored with inactivity, Hemingway soon began writing features for the Toronto *Star.* In 1920, he also worked as a contributing editor of a trade journal in Chicago, where he met Hadley Richardson. The couple married a year later and moved to France. Hemingway traveled through Europe as a foreign correspondent for the Toronto *Star* and spent much time in Paris associating with expatriate American writers such as Gertrude Stein and Ezra Pound. After a brief return to Toronto for the birth of his first son, he quit the *Star* and settled in Paris to become a literary writer.

He published two small volumes of prose and poetry in Paris in 1924 but did not receive attention in the United States until the 1925 publication of *In Our Time,* a collection of short stories. The book—which included the first appearance of Nick Adams, a recurring character who is a typically masculine, but sensitive, "Hemingway hero"—received great critical response for its understated, realistic style. The following year, he published *The Sun Also Rises,* to even greater acclaim. With its depiction of the hopelessness of postwar expatriates, the novel became a definitive rendering of the "lost generation."

Having made his name in Paris, the writer sought new places and experiences. In 1927, he divorced his wife, married Pauline Pfeiffer, and set up house in Key West, Florida. The birth of another son and the suicide of his father took him away from his work, but by 1929 he completed his well-received novel *A Farewell to Arms.* Drawn from his World War I experience, the book portrayed a disillusioned American who deserts the Italian army and tragically loses his lover. While Hemingway continued to spend time in Key West deep-sea fishing, after his last son was born in 1931 he increasingly roamed the world looking for adventure and new material. His nonfiction books *Death in the Afternoon* (1932) and *Green Hills of Africa* (1935) deal with his interests in Spanish bullfights and African big-game hunting, respectively.

Renowned as a sportsman, Hemingway also began to express social and political interests in his writing. His 1937 novel, *To Have and Have Not,* concerns a man who becomes an outlaw to feed his family during the Depression. During the Spanish Civil War (1936–39), he acted on his political beliefs by supporting the Loyalist side and reporting as a war correspondent. *The Fifth Column,* his only full-length play, takes place during the siege of Madrid; the work was published in 1938, along with the short stories from his collections *In Our Time, Men without Women* (1927), and *Winner Take Nothing* (1933). Although the play received little notice, the short stories "The Killers," "The Short Happy Life of Francis Macomber," and "The Snows of Kilimanjaro" among others are still widely appreciated. His Spanish war experience also inspired the 1940 novel *For Whom the Bell Tolls,* a less pessimistic tale emphasizing the brotherhood of mankind.

For the next several years, Hemingway was too busy to publish. After divorcing his second wife, he married Martha Gellhorn and bought an estate called La Finca Vigia outside Havana, Cuba. He spent little time there, however, choosing instead to follow the wars then raging around the world. Before the Japanese attack on Pearl Harbor, he reported from China on the Sino-Japanese War. After the United States entered World War II, he became a war correspondent for *Collier's*. In London, he met journalist Mary Welsh, who later became his fourth wife. From there he ventured to France, where he followed American troops through the Battle of the Bulge and the liberation of Paris. Hemingway became something of a legend, joining the fighting as much as reporting about it.

After the war, he returned to his life of writing and traveling. In 1950, he published *Across the River and into the Trees*, a novel about an aging army colonel that is generally considered inferior to the rest of his work. However, his next book, *The Old Man and the Sea* (1952), received the highest accolades, including a Pulitzer Prize. A chronicle of a fisherman's struggle to catch a huge marlin only to lose it to sharks, the book celebrates man's dignity and endurance as a kind of victory despite defeat. Hemingway experienced a major victory of his own in 1954, when he was awarded the Nobel Prize for literature.

Although in the prime of his life, Hemingway's enjoyment was hindered by ill health. Besides two harrowing plane crashes in Africa, he suffered spells of depression and had to be hospitalized twice at the Mayo Clinic. On July 2, 1961, Hemingway used a shotgun to commit suicide at his home in Ketchum, Idaho.

Hemingway left a lasting legacy. In 1964, *A Moveable Feast*, his memories of Paris, was published, and in 1970, the three-part *Islands in the Stream*, a novel about Bimini and Cuba, was released. His novels continue to be widely studied, and his spare, brutal style remains greatly influential. ✣

Thematic and Structural Analysis

When Ernest Hemingway sat down to write *The Old Man and the Sea,* he was recovering from the worst novel of his career. Critics had attacked *Across the River and into the Trees* as unintentional self-parody, and even Hemingway's defenders had to admit that the book was sentimental and self-indulgent. He was more than fifty years old and had written his last successful novel more than a decade before.

Yet Hemingway had written in the preface to an earlier collection of short stories that

> in going where you have to go, and doing what you have to do, and seeing what you have to see, you dull and blunt the instrument you write with. But I would rather have it bent and dull and know I had to put it on the grindstone again and hammer it into shape and put a whetstone to it, and know that I had something to write about, than to have it bright and shining and nothing to say, or smooth and well-oiled in the closet, but unused.

With *The Old Man and the Sea,* Hemingway put his art to the grindstone and attempted to return to the stylistic precision and apparent simplicity of his earliest short stories while also attempting the bolder measure of putting his career in context. A reader must always be cautious about interpreting a work of fiction as autobiography, but *The Old Man and the Sea* is generally read as Hemingway's attempt to go once again into the deep of his life after a great book, with his only tools being his craft as a writer and the themes that had preoccupied him throughout his career. Such an approach yields a very simple and two-dimensional reading of the novel while slighting the pleasures of the story itself. Nevertheless, in the best passages of *The Old Man and the Sea,* Hemingway uses his skill at description to enrich both the old man's craft and his own, and the work is perhaps most powerful—both as an allegorical story and in its execution—in the way it depicts the Hemingway philosophy that a thing done well and with honor is the only defense against life's absurdities.

Published in the 1 September 1952 issue of *Life* magazine, *The Old Man and the Sea* was an instant—if not unanimous—success, and it was cited specifically in Hemingway's winning the 1954 Nobel Prize in literature. With his suicide in 1961, it proved to be his last completed novel, but more important today, it is generally considered his last great novel.

The opening sentence of the novel (which has no subdivisions) is vintage Hemingway and a marvel of brevity in the way it establishes the main character and his situation: "He was an old man who fished alone in a skiff in the Gulf Stream and he had gone eighty-four days now without taking a fish." The old man, Santiago, had previously worked with a boy, Manolin, but we soon learn that, after the first forty days, the boy's family prevailed upon him to leave the old man and join the crew of a more cautious but also more consistently successful fisherman. The boy, however, continues to look after the old man and to help him with his equipment, including a tattered sail mended with flour sacks, which has the look of "the flag of defeat." At the beginning of the story they meet onshore in their small Cuban village after the old man has just completed his day on the sea.

The initial description of the old man stresses his age, using metaphors of dryness and decay. He is afflicted with a "benevolent" form of skin cancer, and his hands are creased with the scars of his trade, the crevices "as old as erosions in a fishless desert." In contrast, however, Santiago's eyes are "the same color as the sea," with a look that is "cheerful and undefeated," which indicates that he has a rare clarity of vision and a spark of life and intelligence that only death will diminish.

The boy, who apparently is old enough to buy them both a beer on the Terrace, a local bar and restaurant, had learned to fish with the old man from the age of five. He offers to return to the old man's boat, but Santiago tells him to remain with the "lucky" boat, even though that boat does not work the deeper waters, where at that time of year, early autumn, larger fish can be taken. The old man notices that the other fishermen look upon him with sadness, yet he also understands and respects their silence. He accepts Manolin's offer of a beer and of sardines to use as bait the following day, although he makes sure that the boy has not put himself at risk by stealing the sardines. "He was too simple to wonder when he had attained humility," Hemingway writes. "But he knew he had attained it and he knew it was not disgraceful and it carried no loss of true pride." Although he lies to the boy when they arrive at his shack, telling Manolin he has a pot of fish with rice for dinner, the boy knows he is lying. After returning from catching the sardines to find the old man asleep, the boy gets them dinner from the Terrace, and the old man again does not decline.

While eating they discuss American baseball, with Santiago expressing a special appreciation for Joe DiMaggio, the New York Yankees star who had a reputation for doing everything correctly and with an elegant grace. At the time Hemingway was writing the novel, DiMaggio was nearing the end of his career, afflicted with a bone spur in his heel. Santiago seizes on this detail, and for Hemingway it also seems to imply the fatal flaw of all heroes, with reference to Achilles. Santiago and Manolin part, with the old man promising to wake the boy in the morning. Santiago dreams of scenes of Africa remembered from his youth, especially of young lions frolicking on the shore, images he later calls "the main thing that is left."

In the morning the old man goes to the boy's home and wakes him with an apology. "It is what a man must do," responds the boy, who apparently has learned as much about dignity and self-possession from the old man as he has about fishing. He helps the old man carry his gear, and the two have coffee at a place where they have credit. The boy goes to get the sardines and other bait he has promised the old man, and then sees him off with a call of "Good luck old man." Santiago rows out, leaving "the smell of land behind," and he decides that, after fishing the deep wells unsuccessfully the last few days, he will try to find a school of bonito or albacore in the hope of meeting a big fish in their midst. He runs four lines—one at 40 fathoms, one at 75, one at 100, and one at 125—with each carefully rigged so that the bait fish conceals the hook. In what is clearly a self-referential passage for Hemingway, Santiago thinks of the precision he takes in his work and looks inland to see the other boats working closer to the shore. "Only I have no luck any more," he thinks. "It is better to be lucky. But I would rather be exact. Then when luck comes you are ready."

The old man ponders the sea, which he considers feminine, a capricious bestower of great favors and great slights. He sees a Portuguese man-of-war, finding its iridescent bubbles beautiful but thinking of them as "the falsest thing in the sea" because of the filament's ability to inflict pain, both in the water and when removed from a fishing line. Santiago takes pleasure in the thought of turtles eating them.

The flight path of a man-of-war bird leads him first to a school of dolphins feeding on flying fish, then to a school of albacore tuna. The old man hooks one and catches it, thinking to use it later for bait. But then a fish takes one of the deep lines, six hundred feet below the surface, and the old man can tell from the pull of the line that a marlin is taking the bait.

For a moment he thinks the fish has abandoned the bait. Then he feels the line tug again, and when he knows the fish has swallowed the bait he connects the end of the line to two extra coils, giving him extra line in case the fish should run. Now Santiago strikes, "swinging with each arm alternately on the cord with all the strength of his arms and the pivoted weight of his body." Yet the fish responds by remaining deep beneath the surface, moving off slowly and towing the boat to the northwest, out of sight of land. To tie the line off on the edge of the boat might allow the fish to snap it with a rush, so the old man rests it across his shoulders like a heavy burden, arms outstretched—the first of many crucifixion images—slipping a sack underneath the line as something of a cushion. He thinks that, while the fish is large, he has the skill and the knowledge to prevail. When he finds his thoughts drifting to baseball, he reminds himself, "Think of what you are doing. You must do nothing stupid."

The fish pulls on through the end of the day and into the night. "Now we are joined together and have been since noon," Santiago thinks. "And no one to help either one of us." Before dawn, a fish takes one of the other lines, but Santiago cuts it off, as well as the remaining line, and connects the coils in the base of the boat to the line with the marlin, giving him six lines in reserve. At one point, the fish lunges and pulls Santiago's face into the edge of the boat, cutting him below the eye. "Fish," he says aloud, "I love you and respect you very much, but I will kill you dead before this day ends," taking pause to add in his thoughts, "Let us hope so."

He sometimes speaks aloud to himself but is not ashamed of that, and for a reader this increases the impression of Santiago's self-reliance. Yet he wishes the boy were with him, and he is preoccupied with thoughts of loneliness. He thinks of a female marlin he and the boy had once caught, and how its mate would not abandon it. A migrating warbler pauses for a moment at the boat, resting on the line, and the old man thinks of the tough landing that awaits the bird: Hawks often fly out to feed on the warblers as they return to shore.

Another rush by the fish forces him to give line abruptly, cutting his right hand and frightening the bird. He carefully soaks his hand in the water and then decides to eat some of the tuna he has caught, for strength. He cuts it into precise strips, all the while handling the line, and dumps the leftover carcass overboard before noticing that his left hand has begun to cramp. He eats some of the tuna while trying to work the cramp out of his hand, thinking of the cramp as "a treachery of one's own body." Then, as he notices the inclination of the line changing, the fish rises to the surface.

Hemingway describes Santiago's first glimpse of the fish in detail:

> The line rose slowly and steadily and then the surface of the ocean bulged ahead of the boat and the fish came out. He came out unendingly and water poured from his sides. He was bright in the sun and his head and back were dark purple and in the sun the stripes on his sides showed wide and a light lavender. His sword was as long as a baseball bat and tapered like a rapier and he rose his full length from the water and then re-entered it, smoothly, like a diver and the old man saw the great scythe-blade of his tail go under and the line commenced to race out.

Santiago estimates that the marlin is two feet longer than the skiff. While he has caught two marlins weighing more than one thousand pounds in his life, he has never done so alone, and this marlin is the largest he has ever seen. He thinks again that he must outwit the fish. "[T]hank God, they are not as intelligent as we who kill them," he thinks, "although they are more noble and more able." The fish by now has turned to the east, into the direction of the wind and waves, which, Santiago realizes, will slow the fish.

The old man is described as comfortable but suffering, though he does not admit the suffering. Santiago says that he is not religious, but he prays ten Our Fathers and ten Hail Marys, adding, "Blessed Virgin, pray for the death of this fish. Wonderful though he is," and this gives him solace. He baits another line so that he can continue to eat for strength, resolving, "I will show him what a man can do and what a man endures." "The thousand times that he had proved it meant nothing," Hemingway writes. "Now he was proving it again. Each time was a new time and he never thought about the past when he was doing it."

Santiago allows his mind to return to baseball, thinking, "I must be worthy of the great DiMaggio who does all things perfectly." But he is cut short by the thought of sharks: "If sharks come, God pity him [the marlin] and me."

He then recalls one of the great struggles of his life, an arm-wrestling contest in Casablanca against "the great negro from Cienfuegos," at a time when Santiago was considered the local champion. The bout, which had begun in the morning, raged on throughout the day. When Santiago held off a particularly stiff onslaught from his opponent, he knew he had won, and he prevailed the following morning.

Santiago catches a dolphin fish with the extra line, brings it to the boat, then rebaits the hook. While washing his hands afterward he notices that the marlin is pulling the skiff more slowly. As the sun sets, he ponders "his distant friends," the stars, adding aloud, "The fish is my friend too. . . . I have never seen or heard of such a fish. But I must kill him. I am glad we do not have to kill the stars." He briefly feels sorry for the fish, but "his determination to kill him never relaxed in his sorrow for him."

Santiago considers tying his oars across the stern, which would add to the boat's drag and tire the fish. But he decides that "it has reached the time to play for safety." He rests for about two hours to regain his strength. Then he cleans and fillets the dolphin, finding two undigested flying fish inside. The dolphin is distasteful raw, but he eats half of one of the fillets and then one of the flying fish. Then he positions himself carefully, "cramping himself against the line with all of his body, putting all his weight onto his right hand," and falls asleep. At first he dreams not of lions but of a "vast school of porpoises" mating, and then of being at home in bed, with a storm blowing and with his right arm asleep as it cradles his head. Finally he dreams of the lions and is happy.

He awakes with a jolt of the line, as the fish runs and then jumps again and again. The old man has been pulled face down into the slice of dolphin—with implications of the carnage he is trying to inflict—but he keeps pressure on the line as the fish pulls it out, then rights himself. Santiago reaches down to get water to clean the dolphin flesh from his face, fearing "it might nauseate him and he would vomit and lose his strength." His hands are cut, but "pain does not matter to a man," he says aloud.

Having regained his equilibrium, he realizes he must eat to gain sustenance, but he finds the dolphin nauseating. Then, realizing he is becoming light-headed, he remembers the other flying fish and eats it. The marlin, tiring, begins to circle the boat against the resistance of the old man and the line. The old man changes tactics, taking line in, then giving it back as the fish rallies.

The old man begins to see black spots; and while he considers this normal with the exertion, he is worried about feeling faint and dizzy. "I could not fail myself and die on a fish like this," he says. The fish tries hitting the wire leader with its spear, but Santiago keeps strong pressure on the line to discourage it from jumping and thus loosening the hook. Gradually he gains line on the fish, until finally it passes alongside the boat. He sees the marlin "first as a dark shadow that took so long to pass under the boat that he could not believe its length." Santiago finds himself sweating after that, "but from something else besides the sun." "Be calm and strong, old man," he counsels himself. At last he finds, briefly, that he can command the fish, but this lasts only for an instant, and the fish soon resists. The old man tries to bring the fish alongside the boat and then turn it on its side, in order to drive a harpoon into its heart, but time and again the fish resists. "Fish," he says, "you are going to have to die anyway. Do you have to kill me too?" Then he thinks, "You are killing me, fish. . . . But you have a right to. Never have I seen a greater, or more beautiful, or a calmer or more noble thing than you, brother. Come on and kill me. I do not care who kills who."

The old man realizes he is not thinking quite straight, and he repeatedly fails to gain the required leverage on the fish to bring it alongside and turn it. Then, on the seventh pass, with his strength fading, he takes "all his pain and what [is] left of his strength and his long gone pride" and puts "it against the fish's agony." As the fish swims gently on its side by the skiff, the old man traps the line beneath his foot, lifts the harpoon, and drives it into the fish, putting all his weight on it. The fish rises out of the sea and dies in a cascade of water.

Again Hemingway describes in detail the techniques used in lashing the fish to the side of the skiff. At one point Santiago finds himself thinking that the fish weighs fifteen hundred pounds, two-thirds of which should be marketable, at a price of thirty cents a pound, leaving a total take of . . . "I need a pencil for that," he says. "My head is not that clear."

Tying the fish to the side of the boat is "like lashing a much bigger skiff alongside." He rigs the sail and begins moving to the southwest. He thinks of putting out another line for more fish, but he cannot find a lure, and the sardines have spoiled, so he hooks a passing patch of Gulf weed with his gaff and spills from it more than a dozen shrimp, which he eats.

Even so, his thoughts are not quite right. He looks at the fish and feels his back against the stern of the boat as he sails and realizes it was not a dream. Yet he senses "some great strangeness" in the kill, and for a moment he wonders whether he is the one bringing the fish into shore or vice versa. "But they were sailing together lashed side by side and the old man thought, let him bring me in if it pleases him. I am only better than him through trickery and he meant me no harm." Then, after Santiago has been sailing only an hour, a shark finds the skiff.

The sharks in *The Old Man and the Sea* are frequently interpreted as literary critics; the first is a mako, a fearless and unforgiving fish, and, Hemingway writes, "everything about him was beautiful except the jaws." The old man's head has cleared, but though full of resolution he has little hope he can save his catch. "It was too good to last," he thinks. When the shark strikes the marlin, the old man kills it with a stab of his harpoon through the skull. The shark's dying muscle spasms carry it across the water like a "speedboat," and it snaps the rope, thus sinking with the harpoon. Santiago can't bring himself to look at the mutilated marlin. "He took about forty pounds," he says aloud about the shark, then thinks, "He took my harpoon too and all the rope . . . and now my fish bleeds again and there will be others."

"But man is not made for defeat," he says. "A man can be destroyed but not defeated." He knows the sharks will attack again and in greater numbers when he reaches the inner part of the current, but there is "nothing to be done now." Still, he rigs an oar with his knife as a weapon, and he steers on for home, thinking it is a sin not to hope, although his thoughts grow confused and he begins to wonder if it was a sin to kill the marlin. "You think too much, old man," he says. Later he thinks, "Fishing kills me exactly as it keeps me alive."

Soon he spots two more sharks approaching. "*Ay,*" he says, and Hemingway adds in a pointed aside, "There is no translation for this word and perhaps it is just a noise such as a man might make, involuntarily, feeling the nail go through his hands and into the wood." These are shovel-nosed sharks, slightly less fearless but slightly more crafty than the mako; one attacks from underneath as the other attacks from the side. Santiago kills them both, but not before they have done additional damage to the marlin. "I shouldn't have gone out so far, fish," he says. "Neither for you nor for me. I'm sorry, fish." He thinks of the many things he should have brought and now could use, saying to himself, "You give me much good counsel. I'm tired of it."

The marlin is now leaving a trail of blood "as wide as a highway through the sea," and soon another shovel-nosed shark approaches. Santiago kills this one as well, but the knife blade snaps off in the process. "Now they have beaten me," he thinks. "I am too old to club sharks to death. But I will try it as long as I have the oars and the short club and the tiller."

Two more sharks approach just before sunset, and Santiago fights them off with the club. But in the dark he is left practically defenseless. He steers by the light from Havana, but after midnight the sharks come in a pack and the old man sees only "the lines in the water that their fins made and their phosphorescence as they threw themselves on the fish." One shark seizes the club in its jaws and tears it from the old man. He attacks with the tiller, and when it splinters he stabs the last shark of the pack, killing it, but by that time "[t]here was nothing more for them to eat." He is out of breath and tastes blood in his mouth, which briefly frightens him, but then he spits in the ocean, saying, "Eat that, *galanos*. And make a dream you've killed a man." Later, stray sharks "hit the carcass as someone might pick up crumbs from the table."

Santiago can still steer the rudder with the remains of the tiller, and he notices only that the skiff sails better without the huge body of the marlin alongside. The skiff "is sound and not harmed in any way except for the tiller. That is easily replaced," the old man thinks.

"And what beat you," he thinks. "Nothing," he says. "I went out too far." When he sails into the harbor, the lights are out at the Terrace and the village is silent. He pulls the skiff as far up on the rocks as he is able before tying it off. He unsteps the mast and furls the sail and tries to carry it home, and then realizes "the depth of his tiredness." He looks back to see "the great tail of the fish standing up well behind the skiff's stern . . . the white naked line of his backbone and the dark mass of the head with the projecting bill and all the nakedness between."

Seven times the old man either collapses or pauses under the burden of the mast on the way home, again alluding to Christ and the cross, and then after a drink of water he crawls into his bed and goes to sleep "face down on the newspapers with his arms out straight and the palms of his hands up."

In the morning, the boy finds the skiff and the remains of the marlin and goes to check on the old man. Crying unashamedly, he makes his way through the village to the Terrace to get coffee. One fisherman measures the marlin at eighteen feet, and the owner of the Terrace exclaims, "What a fish it was." After returning to watch the old man sleep on, the boy goes out to borrow wood to keep the coffee warm.

> "They beat me, Manolin," Santiago says when he wakes. "They truly beat me."
> "*He* didn't beat you. Not the fish," Manolin replies.
> "No," Santiago says. "Truly. It was afterwards."

The boy knows the old man did everything possible. Santiago asks how the boy fared during the three days he was away, and the boy says they caught four fish but declares, "Now we fish together again." When Santiago says he is not lucky, Manolin responds, "The hell with luck. . . . I'll bring the luck with me." Santiago tells the boy how in the night he "spat something strange and felt something in my chest was broken," but the boy responds, "You must get well fast for there is much that I can learn and you can teach me everything."

Back at the shore, a tourist couple asks about the immense carcass in the water, but when a waiter tries to explain about the marlin and the sharks, the woman says, "I didn't know sharks had such handsome, beautifully formed tails." While "the great fish" is "now just garbage waiting to go out with the tide," Santiago sleeps again and dreams of the lions. All the old man's effort, ability, intelligence, and courage have come to naught. Yet his struggle with the marlin represents a thing done well, and while the achievement might be ultimately absurd, it is in no way insignificant. ✣

—*Ted Cox*

List of Characters

The title *The Old Man and the Sea* might just as well be a list of characters in the novel. The old man, *Santiago,* spends most of the book alone at sea trying to land an eighteen-foot, fifteen-hundred-pound marlin. Yet, while the book does not have many characters, the relationships between Santiago and the characters who exist in the background—as well as between Santiago and the creatures of the sea—are telling.

Foremost among them is *Manolin,* the boy Santiago has taught to fish from the age of five. Manolin is now a young man old enough to buy them both a beer, and it soon becomes apparent that he has learned much from the old man, not only about fishing but also about honor and the proper way for a man to behave.

Only two other residents of the fishing village are referred to by name—a man called *Pedrico,* whom Manolin asks to look after Santiago's skiff, and a certain *Rogelio,* who the old man says would help him catch sardines. Nevertheless, we get glimpses at the kind of people the villagers are. When the boy buys the old man a beer on the Terrace, some of the other old fishermen are sad because he has fallen on hard times, but they do not embarrass him by showing it. Other fishermen poke fun at Santiago, but he is not offended. A local merchant grants the old man and the boy credit on their cups of coffee, and the proprietor of the Terrace expresses awe over the old man's eventual accomplishments with the remark, "What a fish it was." As a whole, the village has the same stoic benevolence as the old man, only without his courage and nobility—none of the other fishermen ventures into the deep waters.

On the other hand, "*the great negro from Cienfuegos,*" whom Santiago defeats at arm wrestling as a younger man, as well as the locals who bet on the match and are eager for it to end in time for them to go to work, are really just other human beings for Santiago to measure himself against.

At sea Santiago speaks to the creatures he encounters, for he relates to them as entities that face some of the same challenges and perils as humans. As a result, the warbler that perches on his line, the beautiful but dangerous Portuguese man-of-war, the sharks, the flying fish, the man-of-war bird, the marlin—and even the lions Santiago dreams of and his "friends" the stars—exist in the novel almost as characters. In marked contrast with Harry Morgan of Hemingway's previous *To Have and Have Not,* whose final words are "a man alone ain't got no bloody chance," Santiago looks off at a flight of ducks and thinks, "[N]o man was ever alone on the sea." ✣

Critical Views

Ernest Hemingway on the Style of *The Old Man and the Sea*

[From the beginning of his career Ernest Hemingway became known as the wielder of a prose style that was spare, compact, and yet full of resonance and symbolic meaning. In this letter upon completing *The Old Man and the Sea,* Hemingway confesses that his short novel exemplifies this style.]

As occupational therapy (joke) while waiting around with bad things happening and no communications I counted word by word the Book IV of the Book that you read from the Mss. (The Old Man and The Sea part). It was *exactly* 26,531 words. My previous count was on an incomplete copy. This is the exact count on the part you read in the same Mss. you read it in.

This is the prose that I have been working for all my life that should read easily and simply and seem short and yet have all the dimensions of the visible world and the world of a man's spirit. It is as good prose as I can write as of now.

—Ernest Hemingway, Letter to Charles Scribner (5 October 1951), *Selected Letters 1917–1961,* ed. Carlos Baker (New York: Scribner's 1981), p. 738

✤

Seymour Krim on the Unoriginality of *The Old Man and the Sea*

[Seymour Krim (1922–1989) was a widely published literary, political, and social critic. Among his books are *Views of a Nearsighted Cannoneer* (1961), *Shake It for the World* (1971), and *You and Me* (1974). In this review of *The Old Man and the Sea,* Krim praises Hemingway for the richness and distinctiveness of his writing but maintains that his new short novel says little that he has not said before.]

Hemingway has things in "common" with Thoreau, Twain, Sherwood Anderson, Gertrude Stein, and no doubt others, as literary historians will soon be pointing out, but still he stands alone. He has written with all the love of which he is capable—the love of men and that of the objects which men must handle, and the physical environment in which they must perforce exist—and this love, or intense feeling if you wish, led him to invent a style which could make the reader *experience* an aspect of life that only came into true being as a result of this one man's art. When you stop to think of it, this is no small achievement; because one man felt more intensely about certain things which the majority of his contemporaries took for granted we were given a fresh art which gave extreme pleasure to many readers and one which was imitated by more American writers than had ever imitated any other of our artists. This is added proof of just how fresh this art of Hemingway's was.

But as *The Old Man and the Sea* shows again, this freshness could not survive too much of a strain—such as frequent publication or "deep" thoughts—without revealing limitations which have become more apparent with each of Hemingway's recent books. This intense and brilliant artist—and we must never forget that he is above all an artist, and quite as intense, though less demonstrative, than Faulkner—has only a smallish range in which he can do his best work, and it is the familiarity of the range which makes his new book (more a long short story than a novel) slightly "old hat."

This is not to say that the book isn't moving, or written and felt with that romantic dignity which has become Hemingway's seal: it is all of that, and it also contains that earnest personal concern with courage in the midst of defeat which has made its author a sort of literary knight of the twentieth century. But the sad fact is that we can anticipate most of the new book as we read it because, by this late date, we know our Hemingway too well. He has paid for his extraordinary celebrity by having been too much with us "too quickly," and he seems to have few mysteries left that we don't already know. By an ironic stroke of fortune we know him almost as well as we know ourselves. ⟨. . .⟩

If history is any guide, Hemingway has already done the significant part of his life's work; it is likely that in the next few years his reputation will go into a rapid decline, to be resurrected much later on when he is read and appreciated by men who are not as close to him as we are and who will see him differently. He is, by our living needs and standards, a true, brilliant, but very limited artist, and I believe that we have gotten all we can from him now. He may write several more good or even fine books of a kind, but it is very doubtful if they will extend our sensibilities and refresh our vision of life as the earlier works did; and the chances are that they will merely repeat or embellish the best of his earlier work, as does *The Old Man and the Sea.*

—Seymour Krim, "Ernest Hemingway: Valor and Defeat," *Commonweal,* 19 September 1952, pp. 584–86

MARK SCHORER ON *THE OLD MAN AND THE SEA* AS FABLE

[Mark Schorer (1908–1977), who taught at Harvard University and the University of California at Berkeley, was a prolific novelist, short story writer, critic, and biographer. He wrote *William Blake: The Politics of Vision* (1946), *Modern British Fiction* (1961), and *Sinclair Lewis: An American Life* (1961). In this review of *The Old Man and the Sea,* Schorer likens the work to a fable or parable in its simplicity, its prose rhythm, and its symbolism.]

The novel is nearly a fable. The best fiction, at its heart, always is, of course, but with his particular diction and syntax, Hemingway's stories approach fable more directly than most, and never so directly as here. It is the quality of his fiction at its very best, the marvelous simplicity of line. (" 'Be calm and strong, old man', he said.") There has been another strain in his fiction, to be sure—his personal ambition to become a character in a tall tale, folklore as opposed to fable. That is the weaker man pushing aside the great novelist. The strain glimmers once in this story, when we are told of the old man's feat of strength in his youth: "They had gone one day and one night with their elbows on a chalk line on the table and their forearms straight up and their hands gripped tight." Take it away.

The true quality of fable is first of all in the style, in the degree of abstraction, which is not only in some ways Biblical but is always tending toward the proverbial rhythm. ("The setting of the sun is a difficult time for fish.") Next, it is in the simplicity of the narrative, and in the beautiful proportion (about three-fourths to one-fourth) of its rise and fall. Finally, of course, it is in the moral significance of the narrative, this fine story of an ancient who goes too far out, "beyond the boundaries of permitted aspiration," as Conrad put it ("You violated your luck when you went too far outside," the old man thinks), and encounters his destiny:

> His choice had been to stay in the deep dark water far out beyond all snares and traps and treacheries. My choice was to go there to find him beyond all people. Beyond all people in the world. Now we are joined together and have been since noon. And no one to help either one of us.

In this isolation, he wins a Conradian victory, which means destruction and triumph. We permit his martyrdom because he has earned it. His sigh is "just a noise such as a man might make, involuntarily, feeling the nail go through his hands and into the wood." He stumbles under the weight of his mast when he carries it across his shoulder, up a hill. He sleeps, finally, "with his arms out straight and the palms of his hands up." There is more than this, and for those who, like this reviewer, believe that Hemingway's art, when it is art, is absolutely incomparable, and that he is unquestionably the greatest craftsman in the American novel in this century, something that is perhaps even more interesting. For this appears to be not only a moral fable, but a parable, and all the controlled passion in the story, all the taut excitement in the prose come, I believe, from the parable. It is an old man catching a fish, yes, but it is also a great artist in the act of mastering his subject, and, more than that, of actually writing about that struggle. Nothing is more important than his craft, and it is beloved; but because it must be struggled with and mastered, it is also a foe, enemy to all self-indulgence, to all looseness of feelings, all laxness of style, all soft pomposities.

> "I am a strange old man."
> "But are you strong enough now for a truly big fish?"
> "I think so. And there are many tricks."

Hemingway, who has always known the tricks, is strong enough now to have mastered his greatest subject. "I could not fail myself and die on a fish like this," the old man reflects. They win together, the great character, the big writer.

—Mark Schorer, "With Grace under Pressure," *New Republic,* October 6, 1952, p. 20

Carlos Baker on Santiago's Christ-like Nature

[Carlos Baker (1909–1987) was the Woodrow Wilson Professor of Literature at Princeton University. He is the author of *Ernest Hemingway: A Life Story* (1969) and the editor of Hemingway's *Selected Letters* (1981). In this extract from his celebrated biographical study *Hemingway: The Writer as Artist,* Baker explores how Santiago may be thought of as a Christ figure in his courage and suffering.]

With awe, Santiago observes that the marlin is two feet longer than the skiff.

But Santiago knows, has known all along, that there are other standards of measurement than feet or inches on steel tape. That morning, at first light, while the boat still moved steadily, inexorable as the tick of time, he had spoken to the fish of his love and respect: "But I will kill you dead before this day ends." It is the huntsman's code—as in the pursuit of the kudu among the green hills of Africa—to admire the courage and the strength of that which one is out to kill. Breakfasting on raw bonito, the old man had reflected that he would like to pass some down to the fish his brother. Yet he knew he must kill the fish and keep strong to do it, and that by the same token the fish's strength must be worn down.

From his new knowledge of "what I have against me" Santiago becomes newly aware of what he has inside him that will enable him to win. It is this sense of proving worth against a worthy adversary which, as much as any other means at his disposal, sustains the old man in his time of stress. The first breaching, like the various slight changes in the slant of the line, suggest that by almost imperceptible degrees Santiago is gaining the advantage. The sight of the fish itself is a further spur, for here at last, expansed before his eyes, is the enormous quarry, the goal towards which he moves. But the chief way in which the power outside enlarges the power inside is through Santiago's resolute comparisons. "Let him think I am more man than I am, and I will be so." Or again: "I will show him what a man can do and what a man endures." If the old man wins, he has proved his own worth to himself once more, which is the proof men need in order to continue with the other and perpetual endurance contest into which birth precipitates them all.

⟨. . .⟩ the zenith of Santiago's struggle, which is also close to the nadir of his strength, comes on the morning of the third day. Now the marlin rises and slowly circles the boat while the old man sweats and strains to get him close enough for harpooning. "You are killing me, fish, the old man thought. But you have a right to. Never have I seen a greater, more beautiful, or a calmer or more noble thing than you, brother. Come on and kill me. I do not care who kills who." But he does care. Though his hands are pulped and he is nearly blind with fatigue, he tries one final time on the ninth circle. "He took all his pain and what was left of his strength and his long gone pride and he put it against the fish's agony and the fish came over onto his side and swam gently on his side, his bill almost touching the planking of the skiff." Now Santiago drives home the harpoon, the fish leaps and falls in death, and the first forty-eight hours are over.

In this movement of the story, as in the phase of the sharks that is yet to come, Santiago bears a significant relationship to other characters in the Hemingway canon. For many years prior to the composition of *The Old Man and The Sea,* Hemingway had interested himself in the proposition that there must be a resemblance, in the nature of things, between Jesus Christ in his human aspect as the Son of Man and those countless and often nameless thousands in the history of Christendom who belong to the category of "good men," and may therefore be seen as disciples of Our Lord, whatever the professed degree of their Christian commitment. The young priest, friend to Lieutenant Henry in *A Farewell to Arms,* is an early example; the old Spaniard Anselmo, friend to Robert Jordan in *For Whom the Bell Tolls,* is a more recent instance.

Santiago shows, in his own right, certain qualities of mind and heart which are clearly associated with the character and personality of Jesus Christ in the Gospel stories. There is the essential gallantry, a kind of militance. There is the staying-power which helps him in his determination to last to the end of whatever is to come. There is the ability to ignore physical pain while concentrating on the larger object which is to be achieved. "Etched on the reader's mind," writes a recent commentator, "is the image of the old man as he settled against the wood of the bow . . . and took his suffering as it came, telling himself, 'Rest gently now against the wood and think of nothing.' " The suffering, the gentleness, and the wood it is noted, "blend magically into an image of Christ on the cross." So it may be. As the old man moves into and through the next phase of his operation, the force of the crucifixion idea is gradually intensified.

—Carlos Baker, *Hemingway: The Writer as Artist* (Princeton: Princeton University Press, 1952; rev. ed. 1956), pp. 297–99

✤

Clinton S. Burhans, Jr., on Santiago as a Tragic Hero

[Clinton S. Burhans, Jr., is a professor of English at Michigan State University and the author of *The Would*

Be Writer (1966). In the following extract, Burhans notes how Santiago is a tragic and heroic figure—one whose own actions result in his inevitable doom.]

Throughout *The Old Man and the Sea,* Santiago is given heroic proportions. He is "a strange old man," still powerful and still wise in all the ways of his trade. After he hooks the great marlin, he fights him with epic skill and endurance, showing "what a man can do and what a man endures." And when the sharks come, he is determined " 'to fight them until I die,' " because he knows that " 'a man is not made for defeat. . . . A man can be destroyed but not defeated.' "

In searching for and in catching his big fish, Santiago gains a deepened insight into himself and into his relationship to the rest of created life—an insight as pervasive and implicit in the old fisherman's experience as it is sudden and explicit in Harry Morgan's. As he sails far out on the sea, Santiago thinks of it "as feminine and as something that gave or withheld great favours, and if she did wild or wicked things it was because she could not help them." For the bird who rests on his line and for other creatures who share with him such a capricious and violent life, the old man feels friendship and love. And when he sees a flight of wild ducks go over, the old man knows "no man was ever alone on the sea."

Santiago comes to feel his deepest love for the creature that he himself hunts and kills, the great fish which he must catch not alone for physical need but even more for his pride and his profession. The great marlin is unlike the other fish which the old man catches; he is a spiritual more than a physical necessity. He is unlike the other fish, too, in that he is a worthy antagonist for the old man, and during his long ordeal, Santiago comes to pity the marlin and then to respect and to love him. In the end he senses that there can be no victory for either in the equal struggle between them, that the conditions which have brought them together have made them one. And so, though he kills the great fish, the old man has come to love him as his equal and his brother; sharing a life which is a capricious mixture of incredible beauty and deadly violence and in which all creatures are both hunter and hunted, they are bound together in its most primal relationship.

Beyond the heroic individualism of Santiago's struggle with the great fish and his fight against the sharks, however, and beyond the love and the brotherhood which he comes to feel for the noble creature he must kill, there is a further dimension in the old man's experience which gives to these their ultimate significance. For in killing the great marlin and in losing him to the sharks, the old man learns the sin into which men inevitably fall by going far out beyond their depth, beyond their true place in life. In the first night of his struggle with the great fish, the old man begins to feel a loneliness and a sense almost of guilt for the way in which he has caught him; and after he has killed the marlin, he feels no pride of accomplishment, no sense of victory. Rather, he seems to feel almost as though he has betrayed the great fish; "I am only better than him through trickery," he thinks, "and he meant me no harm."

Thus, when the sharks come, it is almost as a thing expected, almost as a punishment which the old man brings upon himself in going far out "beyond all people. Beyond all people in the world" and there hooking and killing the great fish. For the coming of the sharks is not a matter of chance nor a stroke of bad luck; "the shark was not an accident." They are the direct result of the old man's action in killing the fish. He has driven his harpoon deep into the marlin's heart, and the blood of the great fish, welling from his heart, leaves a trail of scent which the first shark follows. He tears huge pieces from the marlin's body, causing more blood to seep into the sea and thus attract other sharks; and in killing the first shark, the old man loses his principal weapon, his harpoon. Thus, in winning his struggle with the marlin and in killing him, the old man sets in motion the sequence of events which take from him the great fish whom he has come to love and with whom he identified himself completely. And the old man senses an inevitability in the coming of the sharks, a feeling of guilt which deepens into remorse and regret. "I am sorry that I killed the fish. . ." he thinks, and he tells himself that "You did not kill the fish only to keep alive and to sell for food. . . . You killed him for pride and because you are a fisherman."

—Clinton S. Burhans, Jr., "*The Old Man and the Sea:* Hemingway's Tragic Vision of Man," *American Literature* 31, No. 4 (January 1960): 447–49

✤

Edwin M. Moseley on the Personal Nature of Tragedy in *The Old Man and the Sea*

[Edwin M. Moseley (1916–1978) was a professor at various universities including Washington and Jefferson and Skidmore. He is the author of *F. Scott Fitzgerald: A Critical Essay* (1967) and *Pseudonyms of Christ in the Modern Novel* (1962), from which the following extract is taken. Here, Moseley remarks that *The Old Man and the Sea* is a tragedy of a personal sort without social implications.]

⟨. . .⟩ *The Old Man and the Sea* is very consciously a tragedy in individual rather than in social terms. In Hemingway's story a man does go too far literally in the pursuit of the great marlin, and he goes too far because he has chosen to: "His [the fish's] choice had been to stay in the deep dark water far out beyond all snares and traps and treacheries. My choice was to go there to find him beyond all people. Beyond all people in the world. Now we are joined together and have been since noon. No one to help either of us." All of the elements of tragedy are contained in this bit of introspection: an excess that is nobody's or no thing's fault but one's own choice; a realization of a physical mistake that is nevertheless an example of moral freedom on the part of the excessive man even while he is passionately involved in his excess; an identification with the very thing which he is conventionally fighting; a kind of mature resignation to this vast thing rather than a juvenile spitting at it. The essence of classical tragedy is pointed out in detail after detail dramatizing moral victory out of the physical defeats of personal mutilation, loss of security, and lack of recognition by, say, tourists who can't tell a marlin from a shark. Toward the end of his struggle the old man expresses direct acceptance of the fish as a male life principle in the sea, a female life principle, in a way that reveals a harmony and oneness with the elements of nature and the universe in which and with which he has been struggling. It is as if his final struggle has led to the kind of wisdom that an Oedipus, for example, reaches only through protracted experience and struggling.

A pattern related to the conscious one of the classical tragic mode and structure is the even more conscious one of the old champion and the new champion. This is developed in a number of specific ways. The apprenticeship of the attendant boy is perhaps the chief one. He has learned from the old man, attended him as a kind of devotee or disciple of a god, performing rituals of food, dress, and shelter. But alas, when the old man is at the height of his tragic climax, the boy is elsewhere, and the old man, the tutor, expresses constant need for the young boy, the student. The old man recalls when he himself was the young champion defeating by strength of hand the old champion, the Negro on the coast of Africa, in a contest that drew blood from both the defeated one and himself, ironically weakening his own, the new champion's, hand for some contest in the future. The weakened hand he treats implicitly as his Achilles' heel and relates specifically to the bone spur of Joe DiMaggio, who, like the African Negro, is "a fine man and a great athlete" even in the end of his career as champion. And at the beginning and end of the story the old man dreams of the golden lions in the African sun, which had once been a part of his young, strong experience, but is now only a memory. When the old man lies with his hands mutilated, tired, perhaps sick, perhaps near death, the boy again feeds him and dresses him and pays him homage. The spear of the fish the old man passes to the boy, symbolizing in a kind of double phallic symbol the mutability of virility and the immortality of continuity. Intentionally or not, the imagery recalls the innumerable myths of the sun gods who, in waxing, wane, only to be replaced by other sun gods who will wax and wane, wax and wane, and so on for eternity.

Both the artistic concept of tragedy, in which man gains dignity through suffering, and the mythic structure of the old champion, at his physical end and in a way his spiritual beginning, of course include the Christ pattern. Hemingway's imagery is a broader anthropological imagery, but several references make clear that he utilizes Christ as one symbol among symbols. Chief among these are the mutilated hands, the ambivalent images of blood, the explicit statements of suffering, the carrying of the mast on his shoulders from the boat to his final rest, when he "slept face down . . . with his arms straight and the palms of his hands out." How different from the earlier Hemingway who preached the danger of involvement and the advisability of building a shell against natural emotion. Now in effect he says, Greek-like, that suffering brings wisdom and, Christian-like, that suffering leads to moral victory.

—Edwin M. Moseley, *Pseudonyms of Christ in the Modern Novel: Motifs and Methods* (Pittsburgh: University of Pittsburgh Press, 1962), pp. 206–9

WILLIAM J. HANDY ON SUCCESS AND FAILURE IN *THE OLD MAN AND THE SEA*

[William J. Handy (b. 1918), formerly a professor of English at the University of Oregon, is the author of *Kant and the Southern New Critics* (1963) and *Modern Fiction: A Formalist Approach* (1971). In this extract, Handy believes that *The Old Man and the Sea* presents two different criteria for success, one based upon achievement in practical affairs and the other on inner worth.]

The old man is presented from beginning to end as one who has achieved true existence. His response to every situation is the response of a spiritually fulfilled man. The story, then, is not concerned with the familiar Hemingway search for values; rather it is concerned with the depiction of conflicting values.

Throughout five carefully delineated sections of the novel, the center of focus is always on the image of the old man. The first section concerns the old man and the boy; the second, the old man and the sea; the third, the old man and the marlin; the fourth, the old man and the sharks; the fifth section returns to the old man and the boy.

In the opening section Santiago is shown to be something of a pathetic figure. He is old, alone, except for the friendship of a young boy, and how even dependent to a degree upon the charity of others for his subsistence. His situation is symbolized by the condition of his sail which was 'patched with flour sacks and, furled, it looked like the flag of permanent defeat.' For eighty-four days he had fished without success and had lost his apprentice because the boy's parents had considered him 'salao,' 'the worst form of unlucky.'

But almost at once the tone of the writing changes. Only in external appearances is the old man pathetic. Hemingway reverses the attitude toward the old man in a single stroke:

> Everything about him was old except his eyes and they were the same color as the sea and were cheerful and undefeated.

The contrast in meaning is evident: To be defeated in the business of fishing is not to be a defeated man. The theme begins and ends the novel; never, after the opening lines does the reader regard Santiago as defeated. The point is made emphatic in the final conversation between the old man and the boy:

> 'They beat me, Manolin,' he said. 'They truly beat me.'
> 'He didn't beat you. Not the fish.'

And the old man, whose thoughts have been on a much more profound level of contesting, replies,

> 'No. Truly. It was afterwards.'

The novel's concern, then, is with success and failure, more precisely, with kinds of success and kinds of failure. The central contrast is between the two fundamental levels of achievement: practical success and success in the achievement of one's own being. Similarly the novel posits two kinds of defeat: Failure to compete successfully in a materialistic, opportunistic world where this only is the measure of a man and failure to maintain one's being regardless of external defeat. Thus the real story concerns the meaning, in terms of fundamental human values, of human existence.

Almost at once we become aware that the misleading initial depiction of the old man as a somewhat pathetic figure is the direct result of viewing him only from the standpoint of his recent prolonged ill luck. Had Hemingway continued to present Santiago through the eyes that measure a man's worth merely in terms of his practical success or failure, the novel would necessarily have been a naturalistic one. Santiago's skill, determination, and nobility of spirit would simply have contributed to the greater irony of his finally catching a prize fish only to worsen his lot by losing it.

But the key to all of Hemingway's major characters is never to be found as it is with Dreiser's characters, in merely what happens to them. Rather it is to be found in what they essentially are. This is not to discount the importance in Hemingway of environmental forces, both man-made and cosmic, acting to condition and even to determine human destiny. In fact, those whose values do not follow from the shaping forces of environment are few in number, rarely to be encountered. Santiago is one not determined by environment. And in his age and wisdom and simplicity he constantly reminds himself and the boy, who is learning from him, of the distinction. It is a subtle but vital distinction, one which Santiago never loses sight of. When the boy complains to Santiago about the attitude of his new master, Santiago's response is central to the underlying theme of the novel. The boy points out:

> 'He brings our gear himself. He never wants anyone to carry anything.'
>
> 'We're different,' the old man said.

The real story of *The Old Man and the Sea* begins with this distinction. In the first section two indistinct characters are introduced who embody the values of the practical world, the boy's father and the successful fisherman to whom the boy is assigned. In the old man and the boy's discussion of their enforced separation, we see the old man's simple recognition of the problem.

> "Santiago," the boy said to him as they climbed the bank from where the skiff was hauled up. "I could go with you again. We've made some money."
>
> The old man had taught the boy to fish and the boy loved him.
>
> "No," the old man said. "You're with a lucky boat. Stay with them."
>
> "But remember how you went eighty-seven days without fish and then we caught big ones every day for three weeks."
>
> "I remember," the old man said. "I know you did not leave me because you doubted."
>
> "It was papa made me leave. I am a boy and I must obey him."
>
> "I know," the old man said. "It is quite normal."

But the old man's response means something more than that it is quite normal for a boy to obey his parents; it means the acknowledgment that materialism is the central criterion for action and values in the practical world. And the passage also suggests that the boy has been taught something more than how to fish; he has been taught love and respect, values which he now finds conflicting with the practical demands of his parents.

—William J. Handy, "A New Dimension for the Hero: Santiago of *The Old Man and the Sea," Six Contemporary Novels: Six Introductory Essays in Modern Fiction,* ed. William O. S. Sutherland (Austin: Department of English, University of Texas, 1962), pp. 62–64

✤

Robert W. Lewis, Jr., on Santiago's Solitude and Faith

[Robert W. Lewis, Jr., (b. 1930) is the Chester Fritz Distinguished Professor of English at the University of North Dakota. He has written A Farewell to Arms: *The Art of the Words* (1992) and has edited *Hemingway in Italy and Other Essays* (1990). In this extract from *Hemingway on Love* (1965), Lewis shows how Santiago's solitude and faith result in his spiritual triumph.]

The very first sentence of Santiago's story draws attention to his loneness: "He was an old man who fished alone in a skiff in the Gulf Stream . . ." Although he lives in a fishing village, only Manolin visits him and cares for him. He had even put away the photograph of his dead wife "because it made him too lonely to see it . . .", and for lack of a companion on his boat, he talks to himself and the creatures of the sea. Once he has hooked the marlin, he is towed out of sight of land to do lonely battle, and once he realizes the nobility of the fish he has hooked, he repeatedly wishes for Manolin and thinks, "No one should be alone in their old age. . . . But it is unavoidable." There is a real conflict within him as he ponders his fate and that of the marlin, the strange yet only other friend that he now has: "Now we are joined together. . . . And no one to help either one of us."

Like the other Hemingway heroes, Santiago still has to cope with loneliness, but unlike the others, he realizes that his pride has, in part, brought the loneliness on himself. This knowledge has the power to reverse his feelings; understanding his sin, he masters it. The fertile, feminine undulating waters renew his spirit.

> He looked across the sea and knew how alone he was now. But he could see the prisms in the deep dark water and the line stretching ahead and the strange undulation of the calm. The clouds were building up now for the trade wind and he looked ahead and saw a flight of wild ducks etching themselves against the sky over the water, then blurring, then etching again and he knew no man was even alone on the sea.

Whether he will land the marlin and whether he can keep it from the sharks does not matter to him now. He has *seen.* The persistent use of sight-and-light imagery indicates that the strangeness of the old man is in his supernatural sight, his affinity to the animals that also see well (including the marlin and the horse), and his friendship with the light-giving stars, sun, and moon. He will hope and fight and endure to the limit of his will and strength, but the outcome will not greatly matter as long as he can endure with grace. "Perhaps it was a sin to kill the fish," he thinks, because pride was one reason for his long battle. But loving the marlin is an important extenuation, and if he pays by losing the marlin to the sharks, he can return from his journey into hell (where all the punishment is self-punishment) to live with men. Like Ulysses, Dante, Ishmael, and the Ancient Mariner, a sadder but a wiser man and a teacher of Manolin.

Unlike the real fisherman, the model for Santiago, whose battle ended in a rescue at sea, Santiago is alone even after he reaches port. He beaches his boat late at night, unaided, and carries his cross of a mast alone to his shack. It is only early the next morning that Manolin discovers him and with his tears receives Santiago back into mankind. Once he is within easy range of his home, he thinks, "I cannot be too far out now . . .", but in order for his agony to be complete, being near home and friends is not close enough. He must be completely humiliated before he can emerge from the sea as the new man. Just as the medieval view of love ranged from eros to romanticism to agape and the Franciscan view of the good man as the great lover of God's creation, so does the old man signify the brotherly lover of the marlin, other fish, the stars, the wind, and the very sea itself. "In the Franciscan view . . . man's highest good was the ecstatic union with God, and love alone was the key to this beatitude." The rebaptized Santiago has that key, and it is important to see that the change in him is not in regard to the creatures and elements of nature, but in regard to the rest of humanity as epitomized in Manolin, in Martin, the benevolent owner of the restaurant who gives Manolin food for Santiago, and in other fishermen like his friend Pedro. Throughout the brief narrative, Santiago regards nature as friendly (or evil as are the robber birds and the sharks), and it is only toward his fellow man that he finally knows, like Harry Morgan, that no man alone has a chance.

Pier Francesco Paolini has good points to make on Hemingway's themes, including observations on his Franciscan sentiments, man's ultimate isolation, and the self versus anti-self antithesis that can be seen in the conflicts of the dilettante and the professional (e.g., Harry of "The Snows of Kilimanjaro" versus Santiago), and nihilism versus social consciousness or engagement. The commitment of the Hemingway hero in *For Whom the Bell Tolls* was not completely satisfactory because it was political and partial; the commitment of Santiago "signifies . . . man's creative integration in the drama and mystery of Nature." (Nature, I take it, includes Santiago's human as well as animal and elemental society.)

The Old Man and the Sea is a story of the victory of faith and of the endurance of the man who loves both great and small. No matter what happens to a man, if he can love, he can overcome himself; suffering and even physical isolation will be endurable; man will be "well adjusted" without surrendering his individuality to the tyrannical mass; he will be a part of his world, not an addition to it, not an outlander, not a pitiable excresence on it. He will be no Adam, but neither will he be a feared, outcast Cain. He will love his brother, even as he loves the birds and fish of the sea he loves. He has been a long time learning (if we extend his spiritual chronology back to the youth of the early stories and novels), and eros has helped him learn. Too old for sexual love, eros lives on in him as his dream of the lions of his youth. "Anyone can be a fisherman in May," he says; it takes a strong man to catch the "great fish" of September, the autumn of life. The eros of May or youth is no test for the love of men that outlives eros.

—Robert W. Lewis, Jr., *Hemingway on Love* (Austin: University of Texas Press, 1965), pp. 210–12

BICKFORD SYLVESTER ON SYMBOLISM IN *THE OLD MAN AND THE SEA*

[Bickford Sylvester is a former professor of English at California State College. In this extract, Sylvester traces various uses of symbolism in *The Old Man and the Sea,* particularly the creatures Santiago encounters in the sea and his return to society at the end of the novel.]

A careful study of the behavior of the creatures Santiago encounters at sea reveals an affirmation of the values of strength, total immersion in activity, and the exploitation of adversity. Several species include exceptional individual members whose aggression and desire for intensity of experience lead them to oppose natural manifestations. Thus the great marlin turns against the Gulf Stream as soon as he is hooked, and refuses to yield to the current until the moment of his death. Yet his blue stripes, the color of the sea, reveal that in his paradoxical opposition to the sea he is closer to her than are the brown surface fish who always swim with the current.

Accordingly, the other champions of the story, who each bear the color of the sea, also inherit a defiance of their mother's whims. The blue-eyed Santiago, who has only his hands between himself and the sea (no buoys or machines), only the food the sea proffers, and whose very sun-cancer is significantly benign, also demonstrates that the sea bestows her greatest favors upon those who make their own conditions. Like the marlin, the blue-backed Mako shark who "would do exactly what he wished," and the golden dolphin who shows purple stripes when he is "truly hungry" enough to take any risk, Santiago opposes the sea when her vagaries conflict with his purpose. He crowds the current, and he gladly risks the dangerous hurricane months in which, significantly, the biggest fish are to be had.

Indeed, by a chain of associations pervading the texture of the story, opposition to nature is paradoxically revealed as necessary to vitality in the natural field upon which the action takes place. Both the marlin and the "September" fisherman are old, oriented away from that phase of the life cycle when the natural sources of energy flow freely. But the greater concentration thus required of them yields the greater intensity which is an indication of life itself. All implications accrue, eventually, to expose a fundamental natural principle of harmonious opposition. Hence flow subsidiary motifs which can also best be stated as oxymorons: compassionate violence, comfortable pain, life in death, aged strength, and victorious defeat. These provide the structure of the story.

Each of the exceptional individuals of the various species has something "strange" about his eyes which suggests his perception of the paradoxical logic of nature. Acting accordingly, each adopts a mode of behavior which leads ultimately to his death in an intense contest with a champion from another species. But upon this contact, which always leads to impossible odds for one, depends the vital interplay of nature, as I shall explain presently. "I killed the shark that hit my fish," says Santiago, suggesting the vital round. And Santiago, because of his acceptance of the terrible odds, is able to become "the towing bitt," the essential link, between humanity and the natural world. Christlike, he must "cushion the pull of the line" with his body. Like the marlin, and the Mako who is also part of the scheme, he bears in calm solitude the terrible brunt of the only genuine communion with nature, and thus in his agony he redeems the unextended ones, the shallow water fishermen who make up most of the human race. The parasitical surface fish and the scavenger sharks, of course, fill out the rest of the other two species involved in the circular scheme.

Very subtly, then, the rationale emerges in which Hemingway is at last able to see some transcendent purpose in the stringent individualism he has hitherto regarded, bleakly, as an end in itself. It is a rationale, I think, in which the exceptional performer's position is secure enough to permit his serene acceptance of his fellows. The majority was not born to be like him and yet, dependent upon him, it has its place in the world. Thus, I suggest, we can account for Santiago's compassionate understanding of the shallow water fishermen, without forcing ourselves to ignore the positive emphasis upon exceptional achievement pervasive in the story.

Indeed, it is entirely wrong to regard Santiago's individual experience as valuable only as a lesson in the folly of isolated activity, and to suggest, therefore, that Santiago's reward comes at the end of his journey as he rejoins the community. For Santiago's reward comes, not on land but at the farthest point in his circular voyage, at the moment of his greatest isolation from other men. It comes when he plunges his lance into his quarry.

—Bickford Sylvester, "Hemingway's Extended Vision: *The Old Man and the Sea,*" *PMLA* 81, No. 1 (March 1966): 131–32

SHELDON NORMAN GREBSTEIN ON THE STRUCTURE OF *THE OLD MAN AND THE SEA*

[Sheldon Norman Grebstein (b. 1928) is the president of the State University of New York at Purchase. He is the author of *Sinclair Lewis* (1962) and *John O'Hara* (1966) and the editor of *Perspectives in Contemporary Criticism* (1968). In this extract from *Hemingway's Craft* (1973), Grebstein discusses the structure of *The Old Man and the Sea* and the significance of Santiago's fishing expedition.]

I find no occasion in Hemingway's fiction in which the design is more fully realized in the whole work. In this *nouvelle,* as economical as a short story yet with something of a novel's magnitude of action, we also have an exemplary case of the integration of the outside/inside structure with that of the journey. The sequence of scenes can be described as land/sea/land, imitating the movement of a voyage as it would be made in reality. However, by its place in this sequence each of the elements becomes suggestive of multiple meanings, as does the entire sequence itself.

All the associations evoked by the "inside" in Hemingway's stories, associations both affirmative and negative, here attach themselves to the land. Affirmatively, the land is the locale of Santiago's kinship with the boy, the old man's last and deepest human relationship. The boy tends to the old man's needs as a wife would, reveres him as a son reveres a father, and loves him as a brother or comrade. The land, then, can be equated with family or domesticity, a place of shelter, rest, food, affection, and security. Negatively, and here again are Hemingway's recurrent principles of antithesis and paradox, the land is also the scene of Santiago's disgrace. On land the other fishermen mock or pity Santiago and judge him a failure, with the result that the boy's father forbids him to accompany Santiago. There, too, the old man returns with his skeleton-fish, to be misunderstood by ignorant tourists. It may also be true, as Bickford Sylvester has suggested, that Santiago's return to the shore, exhausted by his struggle with the giant marlin, is the final action of his life—that he has come back to die.

Within the same structural and symbolic pattern the sea also conveys ambivalent meanings, those associated with the outdoors. Affirmatively, it constitutes the scene and condition for man's ultimate experience and his most heroic and intense moment, the combat with great natural forces. Negatively, it is the setting wherein Santiago recognizes himself as erring, sinful, and finally helpless. In nature, outdoors, when Santiago kills the magnificent fish he briefly attains the divine power of taking life; but in nature he is himself overcome by his own mistakes and those ever-present agents of brutish malevolence, the sharks. The sea is beneficent and beautiful. It breeds the creatures man needs for food. It is as thrilling to behold as a lovely woman. It exalts man and calls him out to noble quests. But the sea also entraps man, luring him out only to ruin him.

The voyage structure is, of course, implicit in all of this, but it has further dimensions and analogues. The order of action in Santiago's trip out to sea, his struggle with the marlin, and the subsequent return home, repeats again the basic pattern of the movement toward and away from engagement which we have observed before in Hemingway's fiction. Just as Nick Adams and other Hemingway protagonists are impelled into conflict and retreat from it wounded and disenchanted, so the aged Santiago leaves the shore hopeful, conquers his adversary in mortal combat, then makes a disastrous retreat. The voyage structure also organizes the *nouvelle* into symmetrical parts. The trip out, to the moment of engagement with the fish, occupies the first quarter of the work; the return to land takes up the last quarter. But the destination or purpose of the voyage, the battle itself, appropriately comprises the work's center.

Two other subpatterns are interwoven with the land/sea/land structure and call our attention to its inherent antitheses of the known against the unknown and the human against the infinite. Furthermore, each of these subpatterns reduplicates the three-part structure. These patterns are: together/alone/together, darkness/light/darkness.

In the first of these Santiago leaves the shore, where his intimate comradeship with the boy has been portrayed, ventures out to sea and to the struggle alone, then returns to the renewed and intensified love of the boy. During the long agony of the combat and voyage back, Santiago's reiterated plea "I wish I had the boy" assumes almost the significance of an incantation or leitmotif. By implication, human love and help become man's major resources in the struggle with nature. At the voyage's culmination Santiago's wish comes true: he will indeed have the boy, for as long as he lives. He has earned at least this much.

—Sheldon Norman Grebstein, *Hemingway's Craft* (Carbondale: Southern Illinois University Press, 1973) pp. 22–24

JOSEPH M. FLORA ON PRACTICAL CHRISTIANITY IN *THE OLD MAN AND THE SEA*

> [Joseph M. Flora (b. 1934), a professor of English at the University of North Carolina, is the author of *Hemingway's Nick Adams* (1982) and *Ernest Hemingway: A Study of the Short Fiction* (1989). In this extract, Flora, tracing some of the biblical allusions in *The Old Man and the Sea,* finds the novel asserting the validity of a practical Christianity.]

By emphasizing Santiago's role as one who accepts the challenge of Jesus, we guard against making too much of the parallel at the end of the novella between Santiago and Jesus. It is true that we are pointedly reminded of Jesus' crucifixion at the end of the work, but this likeness should be seen in terms of discipleship. Santiago becomes more like the Christ because he has dared to launch out into the deep. He thereby experiences tremendous victory—but also great loss. *The Old Man and the Sea* is a striking illustration of what is probably one of Frederic Henry's best thoughts in *A Farewell to Arms*: "It is in defeat that we become Christian." Significantly, the young priest of that novel fails to grasp the truth of Frederic's observation. The Church does not give to Hemingway's characters the direction many of them crave. The story of Santiago is an ironic counterpoint to the story of Simon Peter and the other fishermen. It is not that Christianity is irrelevant to man's needs; it is just that Hemingway came increasingly to believe that man must do what he can do alone.

In addition to counterpointing the action of his story with the biblical account of the fishermen, Hemingway has skillfully produced a verbal texture that recalls one of the most famous of New Testament passages, St. Paul's treatise on love in I Corinthians, Chapter 13. The chapter concludes: "And now abideth faith, hope, charity, these three; but the greatest of these is charity." Hemingway has Santiago cherish the same triumvirate and in the same order. Almost immediately Hemingway presents Santiago and the boy together as an embodiment of faith. Speaking of his father, Manolin says, " 'He hasn't much faith.' 'No,' the old man said, 'But we have. Haven't we?' 'Yes,' the boy said." Both the boy's and

Santiago's dreams of lions in Africa symbolize this faith. As faith moves into the realm of action, hope becomes an important element. About the hope so necessary in pursuit Hemingway observes of Santiago as the old man prepares for his trip: "His hope and his confidence had never gone. But now they were freshening as when the breeze rises." Later the sharks sorely try that hope, but Santiago thinks of the great DiMaggio, who with his painful bone spur that has hampered his baseball playing serves to symbolize the hope active in conflict. So Santiago rallies: "He watched only the forward part of the fish and some of his hope returned." "It is silly not to hope, he thought. Besides I believe it is a sin."

Santiago is a compelling character because with his faith and hope, love is closely interwoven: "Most people are heartless about turtles because a turtle's heart will beat for hours after he has been cut up and butchered. But the old man thought, I have such a heart too and my feet and hands are like theirs." Already an important part of the old man, love emerges as the growing part of him, the part that is deepened in the climactic death of the marlin. Santiago's love for the fish is established early: "Fish," he said, "I love you and respect you very much. But I will kill you dead before this day ends." The fish possesses precisely the virtues of Santiago himself, and in the struggle Santiago achieves an at-one-ment with his "victim"; "Never have I seen a greater, or more beautiful, or a calmer or more noble thing than you, brother. Come and kill me. I do not care who kills who." Time is arrested in love as the fish ("which is my brother") dies: "Then the fish came alive, with his death in him, and rose high out of the water showing all his great length and width and all his power and his beauty. He seemed to hang in the air above the old man in the skiff. Then he fell into the water with a crash that sent spray over the old man and over all the skiff." As he prepares to take the fish ashore, Santiago reflects: "I think I felt his heart."

In *The Old Man and the Sea* Hemingway presents a parable of practical Christianity. The theology of Christianity may no longer be valid, but—as Santiago's life illustrates—a practical Christian experience may yet be the best course open to man. To be humble, to endure, to launch out into the deep, to have faith, hope, and love—these achievements are still the most rewarding. *The Old Man and the Sea* illustrates the essence of Christian discipleship and does so in specifically biblical terms.

—Joseph M. Flora, "Biblical Allusion in *The Old Man and the Sea*," *Studies in Short Fiction* 10, No. 2 (Spring 1973): 145–47

✣

LINDA W. WAGNER ON HEMINGWAY'S LANGUAGE

[Linda W. Wagner (b. 1936) is a professor of English at Wayne State University and a prolific literary critic. Among her works are *Hemingway and Faulkner: Inventors, Masters* (1975) and *Ernest Hemingway: A Reference Guide* (1977). In this extract, Wagner explores Hemingway's use of Modernist techniques, notably the paring down of language to the stark essentials.]

In considering each word's significance, the writer was also constrained to create an active, moving focus. Literature could never exist as a static picture. Verbs were prized; adjectives made useful. The Imagists had initially made these suggestions and Pound's work with Chinese ideograms intensified their interest. For Hemingway, the principle of active writing operated at a double level in *The Old Man and the Sea.* There are many verbs and surprisingly few adjectives, considering that much of the novel is description. And, in a broader sense, Santiago's struggle is always a dynamic one. There is movement, verve—even when only the stars are moving. The book's original title (*The Sea in Being*) suggested this dynamism, reflecting the source of Hemingway's later pride as he commented that "the emotion was made with the action." Had Santiago not cared so much, he would not have gone out so far; had he not revered the fish, he would have cut the line and come home; had he not come to love it, he would not have struggled so valiantly to save little more than its carcass. Just as every word in the book is there for a purpose, so is Santiago's every act. His dialogue with his left hand is a vivid reminder of the importance of each gesture, each movement.

By focusing on the immediate action, Hemingway follows Imagist doctrine and also avoids the sentiment inherent in his choice of hero. Santiago is pure pathos—alone except for an unrelated boy, poor, comfortless, unlucky, and old; yet because Hemingway presents him as proud and courageous, aligned with the arch young lions, that is the way we see him. (As Pound commented, the poet can at least partially control his readers' reactions, as the journalist cannot.)

Perhaps this is one of the most difficult of the Imagist tenets to employ, the fact that the author controls without interfering. He presents, he renders the story; but his control is limited to the selection of details. Pound had discussed (in a 1914 essay on Joyce) the dangers of both realism and impressionism:

> There is a very clear demarcation between unnecessary detail and irrelevant detail. An impressionist friend of mine talks to me a good deal about "preparing effects," and on that score he justifies much unnecessary detail, which is not "irrelevant," but which ends by being wearisome. . . .
>
> [Joyce] excels most of the impressionist writers because of his more rigorous selection, because of his exclusion of all unnecessary detail.

Pound's summary tone suggests that anyone can tell when detail is irrelevant, but only the master craftsman—here, Joyce; later, Hemingway—knows the line between necessary (and superfluous) detail. It becomes a matter of both quantity and kind.

Hemingway's choice of the singular noun *shirt* in his brief opening description of Santiago is one such essential detail:

> Once there had been a tinted photograph of his wife on the wall but he had taken it down because it made him too lonely to see it and it was on the shelf in the corner under his clean shirt.

The reader is led quickly through the impressions—a photo, and colored at that, must have been a great tribute to his love; then Hemingway recreates his sadness, in removing the photo; then he reinforces Santiago's poverty: *the* shelf may well have been the only shelf, just as the single shirt was his only change. In one sentence Hemingway has conveyed both Santiago's passion and his poverty.

The same care with detail is even more evident once Santiago is in action, fishing. Many of Hemingway's paragraphs follow the pattern of (1) large narrative statement, then (2) accumulation of reinforcing details, and finally (3) the summary statement that gives the otherwise objective paragraph its determination. When Santiago baits his hooks, Hemingway leaves no question that the old man is expert.

> (1) Before it was really light he had his baits out and was drifting with the current. (2) One bait was down forty fathoms. The second was at seventy-five and the third and fourth were down in the blue water at one hundred and one hundred and twenty-five fathoms. Each bait hung head down with the shank of the hook inside the bait fish, tied and sewed solid and all the projecting part of the hook, the curve and the point, was covered with fresh sardines. Each sardine was hooked through both eyes so that they made a half-garland on the projecting steel. (3) There was no part of the hook that a great fish could feel which was not sweet smelling and good tasting.

The final tone, established through the adjectives "sweet smelling and good tasting," comes as no surprise to the reader, even though he has been reading about baits, because earlier in the description, Hemingway had used the words *solid, fresh,* and particularly *half-garland.* The reader is thus viewing the entire process as Santiago would—the fish are beautifully fresh, the act of fishing is a ritual.

Working in a nearly poetic condensation, Hemingway turns frequently to figures of speech—often patterned in a series—as a way of giving extra meaning to his seemingly simple descriptions. Our initial picture of Santiago depends largely on this use of connected images. We first see his patched sail, looking when furled "like the flag of permanent defeat." Then Hemingway gives us Santiago's scars, "as old as erosions in a fishless desert." *Defeated, fishless*—the images are rapidly taking us one direction until the author moves, quickly, to Santiago's eyes: "Everything about him was old except his eyes and they were the same color as the sea and were cheerful and undefeated." The identification with the sea, coupled with the direct contradiction of "undefeated," establishes the tone Hemingway wants. But we also have the facts—and it is not because of the existing facts that Santiago is whole, but rather because of his spirit.

—Linda W. Wagner, "The Poem of Santiago and Manolin," *Modern Fiction Studies* 19, No. 4 (Winter 1973–74): 518–21

✣

Jogendra Kaushal on Hemingway's Concept of the Artist

[Jogendra Kaushal (b. 1928) is a member of the post-graduate department of English and research at Punjabi University in Patiala, India. He is the author of *Ernest Hemingway: A Critical Study* (1974), from which the following extract is taken. Here, Kaushal maintains that *The Old Man and the Sea* is a figurative depiction of Hemingway's concept of the artist.]

The Old Man and the Sea sets forth Hemingway's concept of the artist and his profession. He always believed that an artist in order to create something truly outstanding must outstep the normal limits and must go far out. Judged from this angle, the book projects an image of Hemingway's determined effort to write his best. Hemingway took his vocation with the same meticulous care, with the same degree of high seriousness and precision as Santiago took his. "Others let them drift with the current", but Santiago "kept them with precision". And he "would rather be exact". This choice of precision, exactitude, minuteness were strictly Hemingway's choices in his profession as writer. He had in him the same reverence for his material as Santiago has for his game, the same code, the same courage, patience, perseverance and endurance. For Hemingway, life was a big game and he would approach it with purity of line, like an excellent huntsman. It was the basic life battle that had tickled the great novelist all through: a brave simple man struggling against unconquerable elemental forces of life. If he can fight them well, then alone will he be entitled to the biggest prize. And *The Old Man and the Sea* was after all Hemingway's biggest prize, the consummation of his art and his final attainment. And after its completion, Hemingway had the same sense of satisfaction as Santiago had after his laboriously won and heroically lost prize.

"All the things that are in it", wrote Hemingway of his masterpiece, "do not show, but only are with you after you have read it. . . . It's as though I had gotten finally what I had been working for all my life".

If the autobiographical interpretation has any validity, *The Old Man and the Sea,* like Shakespeare's *Tempest,* represents Hemingway as winding up his life-long business as writer and handing down his "spear to the boy and the head of marlin to Pedrico so that he could chop it up to use in fish traps". That may be taken as Santiago's last will and testament when he hands down to the new generation the traditions and cumulative wisdom contained in the advice, "The ocean is very big and skiff is small and hard to see. . . ."

Deficient in luck but not in technique, Santiago, the tutor figure speaks of his experience to the younger generation, ready to enter the same capricious sea and to face the same predatory sharks, as is man's destiny:

> "We must get a good killing lance and always have it on board. You can make the blade from a spring leaf from an old Ford. We can grind it in Guanabacoa. It should be sharp and not tempered so it will break. My knife broke."

As the *Tempest* provides a clue to the state of mind in which Shakespeare was so does *The Old Man and the Sea* provide us a glimpse into Hemingway's frame of mind during the last few years of his life. The novel is a key to Hemingway's vision as it finally was. Ostensibly the brightest of his books, *The Old Man and the Sea* is not free from the sense of *nada,* the formidable nothingness that had haunted Hemingway all through. It is amazing to note the number of times the words "darkness", "black", "blackness" and "night" have been referred to in the novel. At the outset of his adventure, "he began to row out in the dark", after they had eaten with no light on the table. A man-of-war bird with his long black wings, the sea with dark water are references in the beginning. Later the marlin was "frightened by something in the night". "For an hour the old man had been seeing black spots before his eyes". The shark came as "the dark cloud of blood". At the end of his long travail "when he sailed into the little harbour the lights of the Terrace were out". On page after page, these references abound. They are not just accidental. This darkness is Hemingway's own "inner gulf of non-meaning", his "Kafka nightmare", an "all enveloping realm of nothingness and night" which he had, all through his life, been trying to avoid and which Santiago has been fighting against day in and day out. But it is significant to note that despite his Promethean struggle, Santiago has not been able to chuck it off. Lord Christ himself could not do it. Darkness in which the human life is engulfed is simply irremoveable. One has to live in the midst of it, in spite of it. The darkness will remain, looming as large for ever, and so will the mysterious sea.

Thus *The Old Man and the Sea,* viewed as the most optimistic of Hemingway's works, has *nada* in the beginning and *'nada'* in the end. "Nor do I think", observed Cleanth Brooks, "that Hemingway in his most recent story now finds the world any more meaningful than he once found it".

The Old Man and the Sea is a story of a magnificent failure. It is a story of splendid success too. But it is failure, the sense of being "truly beaten", that stands out in the end. Once again the winner takes nothing, except a few good words from his descendents who saw Santiago's "footprints on the sands of time". What remains behind is the everlasting angry sea and the rapacious ripping packs of sharks", waiting for still other riders to the sea. What keeps haunting us long after we close the book is the gloomy but not ungenuine observation of the old man.

—Jogendra Kaushal, *Ernest Hemingway: A Critical Study* (New Delhi: Chandi Publishers, 1974), pp. 115–16

Charles Taylor on Hemingway and Nietzsche

[Charles Taylor (b. 1940) is a professor of philosophy at Wright State University and the author of *Hegel* (1975), *Hegel and Modern Society* (1979), and *Philosophical Arguments* (1995). In this extract, Taylor contrasts the prevailing view of *The Old Man and the Sea* as a Christian parable with the notion that the novel embodies elements from the life-affirming philosophy of Friedrich Nietzsche.]

⟨. . .⟩ the message of the parable of Santiago is that he 'went out too far'; Santiago committed a sin for which he must pay—at least this is the traditional reading. What is important to see in this interpretation is that it makes everything intelligible and clear: Santiago committed a sin for which he was punished and then forgiven, he was released from further guilt for having gone out too far. The clarity in this parable is rooted in the Platonic dualistic thinking of Christianity. If we freely choose 'to go out too far' we can only be released from our sins by the grace of a God existing in a separate reality. In reading the tragic parable we, the spectators, experience another aspect of this transparent existence. As Aristotle has told us we are spectators removed totally from the action 'on the stage'; the effect of the drama is the *catharsis* that allows us to get rid of, be released and separated from the evil, suffering and pain of life and return safely to our security. Nietzsche would suggest that this security and transparency are illusory.

We can begin our Nietzschean interpretation of Santiago by pointing out that Santiago, in going so far out, was participating in and therefore affirming life in the highest manner possible. Santiago is tied to the Dionysian throughout the book. In the beginning he says, "I am a strange old man"; Santiago knows that life itself is strange, he pays attention to the ambiguous. From the time he gets into his boat and heads 'far out' his own understanding of life begins to appear more and more clearly. He thinks of the birds:

> Why did they make birds so delicate and fine as those sea swallows when the ocean can be so cruel? She is kind and very beautiful. But she can be so cruel and it comes so suddenly and

> such birds that fly, dipping and hunting, with their small sad voices are made too delicately for the sea.

He thinks of the sea as feminine, expressing his love, and acknowledges the 'bad things,' the hatred which he sees as necessarily tied to any true love. The others who have power boats, those who can separate themselves from the sea, consider it masculine, an enemy or contestant: they either win or lose in the struggle with the 'other.' For Santiago the sea is Dionysian, it gives and withholds great favors. The same contradiction is seen in the Portuguese man-of-war: "The iridescent bubbles [of the Portuguese man-of-war] were beautiful. But they were the falsest thing in the sea. . . ." Santiago, then, thinks of himself, the sea, the birds and the creatures of the sea in terms of one of the two fundamental categories of the Dionysian—the insight into the radical ambiguity of existence.

Santiago also pays much attention to the second basic category of the Dionysian—the unity of all existence. The ideas of solidarity and interdependence are seen throughout the book. An early example of this unity is seen in Santiago's thoughts of turtles:

> Most people are heartless about turtles because a turtle's heart will beat for hours after he has been cut up and butchered. But the old man thought, I have such a heart too and my feet and hands are like theirs. He ate the white eggs to give himself strength. He ate them all through May to be strong in September and October for the truly big fish.

Soon after hooking the marlin Santiago begins to focus on their equality; both are 'strange,' both know how to make their fight:

> Then he began to pity the great fish he had hooked. He is wonderful and strange and who knows how old he is, he thought. Never have I had such a strong fish nor one who acted so strangely. Perhaps he is too wise to jump. He could ruin me by jumping or by a wild rush. But perhaps he has been hooked many times before and he knows that this is how he should make his fight. He cannot know that it is only one man against him, nor that it is an old man. But what a great fish he is and what he will bring in the market if the flesh is good. He took the bait like a male and he pulls like a male and his fight has no panic in it. I wonder if he has any plans or if he is just as desperate as I am?

When the tired warbler lands on his boat Santiago apologizes for not being able to take the bird home by saying he is with a 'friend.' Thoughts of unity predominate until the last of the marlin is devoured by the sharks.

Nietzsche argues that every true tragedy, by creating the Dionysian feeling of the unity of existence, leaves the spectator with the 'metaphysical comfort' that life in spirit of *all* changes is indestructibly powerful and pleasurable. Santiago's thoughts about killing the fish disclose this feeling clearly. Early in his battle with the marlin he says, " 'Fish, I love and respect you very much. But I will kill you dead before this day ends.' " After having seen his fish Santiago becomes even more aware of what he demands of himself.

> '. . . Christ, I did not know he was so big. I'll kill him though,' he said. 'In all his greatness and his glory.' Although it is unjust, he thought. But I will show him what a man can do and what a man endures. 'I told the boy I was a strange old man,' he said. 'Now is when I must prove it.'

Santiago shows us 'what a man can do and what a man endures' when he kills the marlin, that which he most deeply loves and respects. In this process we see the strength and abilities of *both* Santiago and the marlin, and in them begin to understand the profound pleasure one experiences in 'proving oneself.'

—Charles Taylor, *"The Old Man and the Sea:* A Nietzschean Tragic Vision," *Dalhousie Review* 61, No. 4 (Winter 1981–82): 638–40

✤

MARTIN SWAN ON WOMEN IN *THE OLD MAN AND THE SEA*

[Hemingway has frequently been criticized for his condescending treatment of women in his fiction. In this extract, Martin Swan notes that the only woman in *The Old Man and the Sea* is one who tries to demean Santiago's achievement.]

The only real live woman in the story is set up right from the beginning; through a simple misunderstanding, a female American tourist is made to represent the full force of Woman's flippant, uncomprehending, emasculating ridicule of Man's achievement—

> 'What's that?' she asked the waiter and pointed to the long backbone of the great fish that was now just garbage waiting to go out with the tide. 'Tibruron' the waiter said, 'Eshark'. He was meaning to explain what had happened.
>
> 'I didn't know sharks had such handsome, beautifully formed tails.'
>
> 'I didn't either,' her male companion said.

What is particularly damaging about the woman's accidental scorn is that the Marlin, stripped of its flesh, is a phallic symbol now flaccid or 'spent'—all she sees of it or chooses to see of it is "just garbage waiting to go out with the tide". With her limited vision, she is inadvertently ridiculing man's lack of 'staying power', and it is just that kind of ridicule which renders a man impotent.

There are only three more sentences left in the book, and we are therefore left with this embittered image of a woman who understands *nothing* of what the old man's fight, and therefore the book, represents. *The Old Man and the Sea* is a work of craftsmanship—if one is disrespectful of it for certain reasons, one can't underestimate the skill which went into the writing of it. Whatever one values in the book one associates with the old man's achievements, and any reader is unavoidably left on this last page with the image of the insensitive and ignorant woman who destroys it. This wilful and perverse gesture of Hemingway's seems to reflect some kind of desperate paranoia, as if he must destroy his own creation with an imaginary woman rather than leave the field open for a real one to do it. 〈. . .〉

Hemingway's misogyny is of course sufficiently in control to avoid being a physical danger, but the same myth is at work—woman is dangerous to man because of her ability to weaken and emasculate, because of her sinfulness and impurity, because of her "openness to all". Masculinity is an attempt to compensate for the servile enslavement of man to woman, and for the loss of control which woman can provoke. It is an ironic twist that the moral simplicity which allows Hemingway to absorb this myth should for so long have assured *The Old Man and the Sea's* suitability for children. After all, that's how this particular sexual disease gets passed on.

Santiago represents, if you like, the contemporary "green-eyed monster" of misogyny. A 'ripper', misogyny in its most extreme form is perhaps a man not naturally violent, but who listens so seriously and guilelessly to the voice of his generation and his bible that he becomes "perplex'd in the extreme". But Hemingway has chosen to turn our own culture's insidious Iago into a Saint.

—Martin Swan, *The Old Man and the Sea:* Women Taken for Granted," *Visages de la feminité,* ed. A.-J. Bullier and J.-M. Racault (Denis, France: Université de Réunion, 1984), pp. 155–56, 163

ANGEL CAPELLÁN ON SANTIAGO'S SPANISH BACKGROUND

[Angel Capellán is the author of *Hemingway and the Hispanic World* (1985), from which the following extract is taken. Here, Capellán argues that Santiago's Spanish background is critical to our understanding of him as an archetypal hero.]

As the world of *The Old Man and the Sea* is the ultimate model of a primitive environment, so its central character, Santiago, is the culmination not only of all archetypical heroes but also of all American protagonists. It is not difficult to see how directly related he is to our long list of archetypical heroes: Villalta. Pedro Romero, Manual García, the old man in "A Clean Well-Lighted Place," Cayetano, Wilson, the old man at the bridge, Anselmo, and Ara. Again Hemingway's awareness of continuity is manifest in an early draft of the novel. The name of the old fisherman in the fragment is Anselmo, the same as the hero in *For Whom the Bell Tolls.*

Contrary to what most critics have believed, Santiago is also born in Spain, an important factor in our study. Hemingway makes it clear enough:

> He was asleep in a short time and he dreamed of Africa when he was a boy and the long golden beaches and the white beaches, so white they hurt your eyes, and the high capes and the great brown mountains. He lived along that coast now every night and in his dreams he heard the surf roar and saw the native boats come riding through it. He smelled the tar and oakum of the deck as he slept and he smelled the smell of Africa that the land breeze brought at morning.
>
> Usually when he smelled the land breeze he woke up and dressed to go and wake the boy. But tonight the smell of the land breeze came very early and he knew it was too early in his dream and went on dreaming to see the white peaks of the Islands rising from the sea and then he dreamed of the different harbors and roadsteads of the Canary Islands.

Santiago was born in the Canary Islands which, among other things, had given Spain its greatest novelist since Cervantes, Benito Pérez Galdós. Although not specifically stated in the novel, Santiago must have been no less than seventy years old (Anselmo was sixty-eight) and, from the context, he spent his childhood and youth on the islands. Therefore, Santiago lived in Spain in the late part of the nineteenth century. As a boy, he took to the sea on a square-rigger that made the run to and from the western coast of Africa—less than one hundred miles from the island of Lanzarote—where he must have seen the lions he dreams of so frequently. Hemingway found inspiration for the character of Santiago in Carlos Gutiérrez and Gregorio Fuentes, his mates aboard the *Pilar*, both born in the Canary Islands.

It has been frequently noted that the old fisherman is named after Saint James, one of Christ's Apostles, and a fisherman. Yet, many more implications to his name are often overlooked. Hemingway wrote to Bob Brown that his choice of name was not arbitrary. According to tradition, Saint James was the Apostle who introduced Christianity into Iberia from Zaragoza to his supposed burial place, Santiago de Compostela in Galicia. He was also the Apostle who according to a well-known legend, had the visitation of Christ's Mother on the banks of the Ebro outside Caesaraugusta, today's Zaragoza, when he felt discouraged about his task of converting those hardheaded Iberians to Christianity. He later ordered a shrine built around the pillar that the Virgin brought, to honor Our Lady for centuries to come. Santiago, the old fisherman, is the Spaniard who like the Apostle has left his native land to bring the good news of heroic values to the New World. Hemingway must have been aware of these implications, which were so familiar to him, in the choice of a name for his ultimate archetypical hero.

Santiago, like the Hemingway protagonist and many Spanish exiles in real life, emigrated to America and settled in Cuba, thus, becoming the best example of the Universal Man, or Everyman. As a Spaniard, he was also culturally a European, but as a native of the Canary Islands, he was geographically an African. When he settled in Cuba, he became a Cuban and an American, as a significant amount of the Cuban population had done in the first half of the twentieth century. 〈. . .〉

There have been the most diverse interpretations of the symbolism of the old fisherman. Given his archetypical dimensions, he could mean a great deal of things as Hemingway himself suggested. Above anything else, Santiago is the archetypical hero *par excellence,* the greatest quixotic recreation in Hemingway. Sergio H. Bocaz wrote an excellent essay perceptively comparing Don Quixote and Santiago. He notes that they both are "positive men inspired by positive ideals," and "both use nature as the source of all purification and of all roads to primitive innocence." Don Quixote and Santiago are contemplative men who like to live in silence and solitude. Finally, Bocaz adds, "they both not only deal with death, but they do it in a most similar manner. Both authors use the technique of sleep to create their common symbolism, the immortality of Don Quixote and the Old Man."

To Mr. Bocaz' analysis, we may add that both Don Quixote and Santiago are proud men and dignified in their manner. They show unlimited courage and no defeat can destroy their moral stamina, even if they lie down after the battle with their broken bones as Don Quixote does, or with their hands and shoulders aching from the fight as Santiago does. They both face with staunch faith and hope the monsters of nature, imaginary or real. They fight with unremitting valor and discipline. Eventually, they are overcome in their struggle, but neither is ever truly defeated. Finally, Don Quixote and the Old Man are both good-natured teachers of Sancho and Manolín respectively.

—Angel Capellán, *Hemingway and the Hispanic World* (Ann Arbor, MI: UMI Research Press, 1985), pp. 109–11

GERRY BRENNER ON FABLE AND FANTASY IN *THE OLD MAN AND THE SEA*

[Gerry Brenner (b. 1937), a professor of English at the University of Montana, has written *Concealments in Hemingway's Works* (1983) and The Old Man and the Sea: *Story of a Common Man* (1991), from which the following extract is taken. Here, Brenner points out that *The Old Man and the Sea* can be read as a fable or as fantasy, and that its scope ought not to be restricted to the realistic interpretation Hemingway himself asserted.]

Old Man has one ingredient common to all variations of the fable—the moral tag, a pithy sentence that underscores the imbedded message of the narrative. Readers can listen to Santiago's repeated self-admonishment, "Don't go too far out," and either accept or scorn parental cautions not to trespass conventional behavior and safe norms. They can also conclude that those who persevere in times of trial and keep their faith under duress will receive their due rewards or that resourcefulness sometimes leads to the sin of pride. Readers can even accept the equations that *Life's* editorial staff offered in a preface to the magazine publication of the novella: Santiago is the aged author Hemingway, the marlin is his noble and beautiful works, and the sharks are the predatory critics and reviewers who mutilate his work and reputation. Other allegorists may see the narrative as a Western saga of humanity's recurrent battle against natural forces that test personal worth and validate the right to existence; or as Everyman's struggle with the Female Principle, as embodied in the sea and its agents; or, finally, as a psychological battle within a self-contradictory human whose actions reveal noble and ignoble impulses. As fraternal fisherman Santiago is Brother's keeper to the marlin he repeatedly calls his brother, but as the marlin's killer Santiago is Cain the fratricide, who here exhibits the carcass of the mutilated marlin to prove his own prowess to villagers who regarded him a luckless has-been.

The wishes and anxieties that undergird fantasy are evident in the text's portrayal of lengthy combat between a puny man and an oversized fish. The confrontation shares the gigantism common to frontier tall tales (Davy Crockett wrestling with huge crocodiles and Pecos Bill taming a 30-foot-tall grizzly bear for his horse) and fairy tales (thimble-sized Tom Thumb swaggering his way through ordinary events, and Jack in the Beanstalk slaying a giant ogre). Such exaggeration satisfies the conventional human wish to perform in larger-than-life ways in an encounter with a colossal opponent or against seemingly insurmountable odds. Santiago's capacity to subdue an 18-foot marlin and lash it to the side of a 16-foot skiff feeds our imaginative capacity to wonder, marvel, and be awed—a primary virtue of all fairy tales.

Likewise, Santiago's exploits call to mind the mythic adventures of Jonah, David and Goliath, Prometheus, Perseus, Tristan, Beowulf, St. George, Gawain, Gilgamesh, King Kong, and various contemporary intergalactic heroes. In all of these tales a person grapples with outsized adversaries ranging from animals to gods and becomes archetypal by silhouetting the human struggle to find meaning within self, society, and the cosmos, a struggle that Santiago enacts in his three-day ordeal. Santiago's voyage, ordeal, and return replicate the traditional pattern of the hero's journey-initiation-return cycle: the hero's journey is community-inspired; his initiation (slaying the dragon, for example) releases reservoirs of vitality needed by his disintegrating community; and his return restores to his community some wisdom that benefits its renewal. ⟨. . .⟩

Despite possible readings of the novella as fable and fantasy, Hemingway's own words dismiss all but a reading as realistic fiction: "I tried to make a real old man, a real boy, a real sea and a real fish and real sharks." This is a forthright declaration of an author's intent, but it can be misleading to read any text according to an author's declared or implied intent. Readers learn to be wary of authors who declare their intentions, if only because as professional storytellers any utterance from their mouths or pens or typewriters or computers may be sheer fabrication. In addition, authors' conscious intentions may be at odds with the unconscious patterns their narratives reveal to readers but from the authors themselves, and so the meanings found in their texts may be quite at odds with what they tried to do. Finally, authors' intentions have limited power over the cultural perspectives, ideological backgrounds, reading strategies, literary experiences, historical predispositions, personal biases, and other factors that contribute to the value—or lack of value—readers find in texts. An author's text controls literally *what* we read, but it has less influence over *how* we read and interpret it.

It is always a reader's task to construct meaning, assign significance, and resolve matters to his or her satisfaction, and different readers—fabulists, fantasists, and fictionalists—construct different meanings and resolve issues differently than others do. It follows that a masterwork is a text that generates a wide array of divergent readings. I think that a mark of the stature of *The Old Man and the Sea* as a masterwork lies in its multiplicity of readings, regardless of whether Ernest Hemingway, a literary critic, or a high school teacher would uniformly agree on those readings as entirely sound or respectable.

—Gerry Brenner, The Old Man and the Sea: *Story of a Common Man* (New York: Twayne, 1991), pp. 9–13

✤

JAMES MELLARD ON HEMINGWAY AND HOMER

[James Mellard (b. 1938) is a professor of English at Northern Illinois University. He has written *The Exploded Form: The Modernist Novel in America* (1980), *Doing Tropology: Analysis of Narrative*

Discourse (1987), and *Using Lacan, Reading Fiction* (1991). In this extract, Mellard notes that the style of *The Old Man and the Sea* is similar to the techniques of oral composition in the Homeric poems.]

Whether because he is imitating Homer or following the rules of a newspaper's style sheet in the heroic tale of old Santiago, Hemingway exhibits on two levels the two features scholars of the oral tradition associate with its defining style: economy and scope. The two levels are defined by what we may label diction and plot. The first operates on the microlevel at the instance of the word, phrase, verse, and passage. G. S. Kirk writes:

> It is now generally agreed that oral poetry tends to develop a conventional phraseology, amounting in many cases to a systematic corpus of phrases for different characters, objects and functions, much more markedly than literate poetry or ordinary speech; and that a highly developed system like the Homeric one maintains both remarkable coverage ("scope") and remarkable avoidance of duplication ("economy" or "thrift") in the creation, preservation and deployment of these fixed, traditional or conventional phrases known as formulas.

The second level is a macrolevel of emplotment that includes events of every sort, ranging from the apparently incidental to the most crucial motifs of whole plots. Mark W. Edwards observes:

> Any reader of Homer notices not only the recurrent formulaic adjectives but also the repeated scenes of performing a sacrifice, preparing and eating a meal, fighting a single combat in the midst of the general battle, receiving a visit from a deity, and so on. Actually these type-scenes, as they are called, are all-pervasive, and as important a tradition of epic composition as the formulae that make up the verses.

These then are the two essential levels of oral compositions. "There is," says Kirk in summary, "a wider dimension of the formula style which includes traditional verses and even passages, or, more loosely, conventional motifs and themes; and a narrower one which occasionally affects even single words; but the fixed phrases or word-groups are the most revealing in the first instance." Both these levels operate in *The Old Man and the Sea.* While the second level, what amounts to emplotment, may signal the proximity of a narrative to an oral tradition, only the first pertains to style as such, so in the context of Morgan's study I shall look mainly at the level of diction alone.

The dominant stylistic principle is economy. Economy expresses the need of the oral composer of narratives to fill verbal slots quickly and efficiently (after all, the singer is working without a net before a listening audience). But it is not the poet who refines the word hoard; it is the tradition itself. "This process of refinement," says Kirk, consisted in the rejection of the otiose—the merely decorative alternative—and the consolidation and expansion of whatever was functional and organic. The refinement expressing the principle of economy occurs in the generation of the formulas that define the tradition. In Homer the formulas are noticeable most readily in the recurrent epithets such as "goodly Odysseus," "many-counselled Odysseus," and "gleaming-helmeted Hector." While recognizing that an author imitating an oral mode of narration in effect creates his or her own "tradition," we see that Hemingway's "economy" is most noticeable in such identifying epithets as "the big fish," "the great fish," "the truly big fish," "the great DiMaggio," "the great Negro from Cienfeugos," and other—to our eyes "peculiar"—locutions such as "the Indians of Cleveland," "the Tigers of Detroit," and "the Yankees of New York." Morgan points out other sets of epithets created by Hemingway that give a sense of the oral traditional style. Calling these epithets "adjectives of essence" in both Homer and Hemingway, Morgan notes that Homer's "loud-roaring" or "wine-dark" sea is strikingly parallel to Hemingway's "mile deep" sea and the series involving the "blue," "dark blue," "dark," and "deep dark" sea. Quite rightly, she suggests that these "function as the equivalent of conventional epithets" that readers, as much as Homer's audience, would come to expect in Hemingway's text.

But, besides the epithets, there is another, even more pervasive economy at work in Hemingway's self-selected lexicon for this tale. The recurrent epithets exhibit it in the reuse or recombination of just the same few words. It is exhibited in other ways. For example, as C. P. Heaton has shown, Hemingway employs no elegant variation in the way he tags speech. Heaton notes that Hemingway uses the verb *said* in 170 of the 184 occurrences of a "he said" situation. "When he does choose to use another word, the choice is forced upon him, if he is to express his idea with clarity," as in the eight instances he used "asked" to tag verbalized questions. It is not that Hemingway or his protagonist, Santiago, is unimaginative; rather, it is that the traditional oral mode of presentation Hemingway imitates or recreates in *The Old Man and the Sea* demands such economy of phrasing. Though it is an economy that scholars prior to Parry and Lord tended to regard negatively, labeling it dross, cliché, or *mere* repetition, *mere* formula, without any real awareness of the centrality of *the* formulaic to the entire tradition's existence, it is also an economy, Heaton contends, that produces precise values of clarity, directness, and forcefulness.

—James Mellard, "Homer, Hemingway, and the Oral Tradition," *Style* 26, No. 1 (Spring 1992): 133–35

✤

Thomas Hermann on Hemingway and Cézanne

[Thomas Hermann is an assistant lecturer at the English seminar at the University of Zurich. In this extract (part of his Ph.D. dissertation on Hemingway and the visual arts), Hermann finds parallels between Hemingway's prose and the technique of the French painter Paul Cézanne (1839–1906).]

How did both the artist and the writer succeed in evoking such a feeling of depth by only presenting the surface in their paintings and texts? The answer could be by strictly subjecting all elements to the *motif* or the narrative context, respectively. An individual patch of color (*tache*) does not represent anything read or clearly defined. It becomes significant only in the context of the pictures, and due to its highly abstract nature, it often becomes ambiguous or multi-dimensional. Thus, as Gottfried Boehm has pointed out in his study of the Sainte Victoire pictures, "the same patch of color can evoke the wall of a building, the immateriality of light, a contrast demonstrating depth, the aura of a landscape, etc." Cézanne was fully aware of the importance that was given to the exact placing of such meaningless patches in relation to the whole. To Vollard he said: "You know, Monsieur Vollard, if I placed anything accidentally, I would be forced to redo the whole picture from this point."

Besides closely interweaving single elements, Cézanne made use of other context-oriented strategies. Sometimes he only hints at things, other things are left out completely and, especially in many watercolors, whole areas of the sheet are left untouched, and it is the contemplator's job to recreate them in his or her imagination. Through such deletions, the things represented gain simplicity and at the same time intensity.

By introducing natural symbols, the context can carry meaning on yet another level. Thus, in order to introduce a religious motif, say of resurrection, into a group of bathers, Cézanne would never use a traditional symbol such as a cross. However, he might arrange trees, which are part of the landscape, in such a way that a horizontal branch of a tree crosses with a cypress, thus providing the symbolic meaning without actually using the Christian symbol but by making use of inherent contextual elements.

If we stay with the cliché of the cross, we can see that Hemingway does exactly the same when he has Santiago walk up to his shack after the unsuccessful fishing expedition with a mast across his shoulder. Although several parallels to the crucifixion could be drawn, neither the word *cross* is used nor are there any overt allusions.

> He started to climb again and at the top he fell and lay for some time with the mast across his shoulder. . . . Inside the shack he leaned the mast against the wall. . . . Then he lay down on the bed . . . and he slept face down on the newspapers with his arms out straight and the palms of his hands up.

In Hemingway's prose the context is further intensified by the use of strictly denotative words which, free of any traditional connotations, share a similarity to Cézanne's color patches and by their relative meaninglessness are made open to new and different interpretations. Taken out of their context, the three nouns in the following sentence of part two of "Big Two-Hearted River": "There was the meadow, the river and the swamp" appear almost accidental. But we all know, of course, that within the story these three nouns function as key words.

Hemingway was convinced that an author can delete the most important things from his story, provided he knows enough about what he is deleting. Thus, his readers are invited to fill in the white spots of a story. They will then come to realize that only on the surface is "Big Two-Hearted River" a story about a young man who goes fishing in a fine landscape. The psychological subtext is about the protagonist's problems of coming to terms with his recent traumatic war experience. Being familiar with the carefully structured stories and the often praised terse style, we can understand the young Hemingway who in fear of editorial changes in his texts wrote the famous lines to Horace Liveright in March 1925: "The stories are written so tight and so hard that the alteration of a word can throw an entire story out of key." It is possible that when writing these lines Hemingway had the above-quoted sentence by Cézanne in mind—that if anything was accidentally added to the picture, he would have to start again from scratch. In any case, these two quotations show how much weight was given to placing the right word or patch of color at the right place. Only in this way can the appropriate emotions be evoked in the reader or contemplator.

—Thomas Hermann, "Formal Analogies in the Texts and Paintings of Ernest Hemingway and Paul Cézanne," *Hemingway Repossessed,* ed. Kenneth Rosen (Westport, CT: Praeger, 1994), pp. 31–33

Works by Ernest Hemingway

Three Stories & Ten Poems. 1923.

in our time. 1924

In Our Time: Stories. 1925.

The Torrents of Spring: A Romantic Novel in Honor of the Passing of a Great Race. 1926.

Today Is Friday. 1926.

The Sun Also Rises. 1926.

Men without Women. 1927.

A Farewell to Arms. 1929.

Death in the Afternoon. 1932.

God Rest You Merry Gentlemen. 1933.

Winner Take Nothing. 1933.

Green Hills of Africa. 1935.

To Have and Have Not. 1937.

The Spanish Earth. 1938.

The Fifth Column and the First Forty-nine Stories. 1938.

For Whom the Bell Tolls. 1940.

Men at War: The Best War Stories of All Time (editor). 1942.

Voyage to Victory: An Eye-witness Report of the Battle for a Normandy Beachhead. 1944.

The Portable Hemingway. Ed. Malcolm Cowley. 1944.

Selected Short Stories. c. 1945.

The Essential Hemingway. 1947.

Across the River and into the Trees. 1950.

The Old Man and the Sea. 1952.

The Hemingway Reader. Ed. Charles Poore. 1953.

Two Christmas Tales. 1959.

Collected Poems. 1960.

The Snows of Kilimanjaro and Other Stories. 1961.

The Wild Years. Ed. Gene Z. Hanrahan. 1962.

A Moveable Feast. 1964.

By-Line: Ernest Hemingway: Selected Articles and Dispatches of Four Decades. Ed. William White. 1967.

The Fifth Column and Four Stories of the Spanish Civil War. 1969.

Ernest Hemingway, Cub Reporter. Ed. Matthew J. Bruccoli. 1970.

Islands in the Stream. 1970.

Ernest Hemingway's Apprenticeship: Oak Park 1916–1917. Ed. Matthew J. Bruccoli. 1971.

The Nick Adams Stories. 1972.

88 Poems. Ed. Nicholas Gerogiannis. 1979, 1992 (as *Complete Poems*).

Selected Letters 1917–1961. Ed. Carlos Baker. 1981.

The Dangerous Summer. 1985.

Dateline, Toronto: Hemingway's Complete Toronto Star *Dispatches, 1920–1924.* Ed. William White. 1985.

The Garden of Eden. 1986.

Complete Short Stories. 1987.

Remembering Spain: Hemingway's Civil War Eulogy and the Veterans of the Abraham Lincoln Brigade. Ed. Cary Nelson. 1994.

Works about Ernest Hemingway and *The Old Man and the Sea*

Baker, Sheridan. *Ernest Hemingway: An Introduction and Interpretation.* New York: Holt, Rinehart, 1967.

Baskett, Sam S. "Toward a 'Fifth Dimension' in *The Old Man and the Sea.*" *Centennial Review* 19 (1975): 269–86.

———. "The Great Santiago: Opium, Vocation, and Dream in *The Old Man and the Sea.*" *Fitzgerald/Hemingway Annual,* 1976, pp. 230–42.

Benson, Jackson J. *Hemingway: The Writer's Art of Self-Defense.* Minneapolis: University of Minnesota Press, 1969.

Bradford, M. E. "On the Importance of Discovering God: Faulkner and Hemingway's *The Old Man and the Sea.*" *Mississippi Quarterly* 20 (1967): 158–62.

Brenner, Gerry. *Concealments in Hemingway's Works.* Columbus: Ohio State University Press, 1983.

Cooper, Stephen. *The Politics of Ernest Hemingway.* Ann Arbor, MI: UMI Research Press, 1987.

Cooperman, Stanley. "Hemingway and Old Age: Santiago as Priest of Time." *College English* 27 (1965–66): 388–91.

Culver, Michael. "Sparring in the Dark: Hemingway, Strater and *The Old Man and the Sea.*" *Hemingway Review* 11, No. 2 (Spring 1992): 31–37.

Denis, Brian. *The True Gen: An Intimate Portrait of Ernest Hemingway by Those Who Knew Him.* New York: Grove Press, 1988.

Donaldson, Scott. *By Force of Will: The Life and Art of Ernest Hemingway.* New York: Viking, 1977.

Fleming, Robert E. *The Face in the Mirror: Hemingway's Writers.* Tuscaloosa: University of Alabama Press, 1994.

Gurko, Leo. *Ernest Hemingway and the Pursuit of Heroism.* New York: Crowell, 1968.

Halverson, John. "Christian Resonance in *The Old Man and the Sea.*" *Modern Language Notes* 2 (1964): 50–54.

Hamilton, John Bowen. "Hemingway and the Christian Paradox." *Renascence* 24 (1972): 141–54.

Harlow, Benjamin C. "Some Archetypal Motifs in *The Old Man and the Sea.*" *McNeese Review* 17 (1966): 74–79.

Hays, Peter L. *Ernest Hemingway.* New York: Continuum, 1990.

Heaton, C. P. "Style in *The Old Man and the Sea.*" *Style* 4 (1970): 11–27.

Hofling, Charles K. "Hemingway's *The Old Man and the Sea* and the Male Reader." *American Imago* 20 (1963): 161–73.

Hovey, Richard B. *Hemingway: The Inward Terrain.* Seattle: University of Washington Press, 1968.

Johnston, Kenneth G. "The Star in Hemingway's *The Old Man and the Sea.*" *American Literature* 42 (1970): 388–91.

Killinger, John. *Hemingway and the Dead Gods: A Study in Existentialism.* Lexington: University of Kentucky Press, 1961.

Lee, A. Robert, ed. *Ernest Hemingway: New Critical Essays.* Totowa, N.J.: Barnes & Noble, 1983.

Lewis, Robert W. *Hemingway in Italy and Other Essays.* New York: Praeger, 1990.

Lynn, Kenneth S. *Hemingway.* New York: Simon & Schuster, 1987.

Mansell, Darrel. "When Did Hemingway Write *The Old Man and the Sea?*" *Fitzgerald/Hemingway Annual,* 1975, pp. 311–24.

Mellow, James R. *Hemingway: A Life without Consequences.* Boston: Houghton Mifflin, 1992.

Messent, Peter B. *Ernest Hemingway.* New York: St. Martin's Press, 1992.

Monteiro, George. "Santiago, DiMaggio, and Hemingway: The Ageing Professionals of *The Old Man and the Sea.*" *Fitzgerald/Hemingway Annual,* 1975, pp. 273–80.

Morgan, Kathleen, and Luis Losada. "Santiago in *The Old Man and the Sea:* A Homeric Hero." *Hemingway Review* 12, No. 1 (Fall 1992): 35–51.

Nagel, James, ed. *Ernest Hemingway: The Writer in Context.* Madison: University of Wisconsin Press, 1984.

Noble, Donald R., ed. *Hemingway: A Revaluation.* Troy, NY: Whitston, 1983.

Pettite, Joseph. "Hemingway and Existential Education." *Journal of Evolutionary Psychology* 12 (1991): 152–64.

Prizel, Yuri. "The Critics and *The Old Man and the Sea.*" *Research Studies* 41 (1973): 208–16.

Rosen, Kenneth, ed. *Hemingway Repossessed.* Westport, CT: Praeger, 1994.

Rovit, Earl. *Ernest Hemingway.* New York: Twayne, 1963.

Rubinstein, Annette T. "Brave and Baffled Hunter." *Mainstream* 13 (1960): 1–23.

Scafella, Frank, ed. *Hemingway: Essays of Reassessment.* New York: Oxford University Press, 1991.

Sylvester, Bickford. " 'They Went Through This Fiction Every Day': Informed Illusion in *The Old Man and the Sea.*" *Modern Fiction Studies* 12 (1966): 473–77.

Timms, David. "Contrasts in Form: Hemingway's *The Old Man and the Sea* and Faulkner's *The Bear.*" In *The Modern American Novella,* ed. A. Robert Lee. New York: St. Martin's Press, 1989, pp. 97–112.

Toynbee, Philip. "Hemingway." *Encounter* 17, No. 4 (October 1961): 86–88.

Wagner, Linda W., ed. *Ernest Hemingway: Six Decades of Criticism.* East Lansing: Michigan State University Press, 1987.

Waldhorn, Arthur. *A Reader's Guide to Ernest Hemingway.* New York: Farrar, Straus & Giroux, 1972.

Watson, William Braasch. "Investigating Hemingway." *North Dakota Review* 60 (1992): 1–27.

Weber, Ronald. *Hemingway's Art of Non-fiction.* New York: St. Martin's Press, 1990.

Weeks, Robert P. "Fakery in *The Old Man and the Sea.*" *College English* 24 (1962–63): 188–92.

Wells, Arvin R. "A Ritual of Transfiguration: *The Old Man and the Sea.*" *University Review* 30 (1963–64): 95–101.

Williams, Wirt. *The Tragic Art of Ernest Hemingway.* Baton Rouge: Louisiana State University Press, 1981.

Wylder, Delbert E. *Hemingway's Heroes.* Albuquerque: University of New Mexico Press, 1969.

Young, Philip. *Ernest Hemingway: A Reconsideration.* University Park: Pennsylvania State University Press, 1966.

Index of Themes and Ideas

ACROSS THE RIVER AND INTO THE TREES, and how it compares, 11

"BIG TWO-HEARTED RIVER," and how it compares, 67–68

BROTHERHOOD, as theme, 40, 42–45, 62

CÉZANNE, Hemingway compared to, 66–68

CONTINUITY, as theme, 34

COURAGE, as theme, 25, 28–30, 61

DEATH IN THE AFTERNOON, and how it compares, 6–7

DIGNITY, as theme, 25, 60

DIMAGGIO, JOE, and his role in the novel, 6, 13, 16, 34, 47

DON QUIXOTE (Cervantes), and how it compares, 60–61

ENDURANCE, as theme, 16, 19, 30, 31, 40, 47, 51, 60–61, 63

FAREWELL TO ARMS, A, and how it compares, 30, 46

FOR WHOM THE BELL TOLLS, and how it compares, 30, 40, 58

HEMINGWAY, ERNEST: life of, 8–10; limited range of, 24–26; suicide of, 10, 12

HOMER, Hemingway compared to, 64–66

HONOR, as theme, 11, 22

HOPE, as theme, 46–47

LAND, as symbol, 43–44

LIONS, as symbols, 6, 13, 17, 21, 23, 40, 47, 49, 59

LOVE, as theme, 47–48

MANOLIN: as new champion, 34; and his role in the novel, 12–13, 21, 22, 35, 49; as Santiago's disciple, 37–38, 39, 46–47, 52, 61; as substitute son, 6; 44

MARLIN: as a bull, 6–7; as phallic symbol, 34, 57; and its role in the novel, 14–21, 41; as Santiago's brother, 18, 31, 33, 38–39, 41; Santiago's love for, 15, 16, 31, 39, 47–48, 55

MOBY-DICK (Melville), and how it compares, 6–7

OLD MAN AND THE SEA, THE: action in, 48–51; art of omission in, 5, 67–68; as autobiography, 5–6; 11, 13–14, 28, 51–53, 63; biblical allusion in, 46–48, 59–60; darkness in, 52–53; detail in, 48–51; as fable, 26–28, 61–63; as fantasy, 61–63; harmonious opposition in, 41–43; and Hemingway's intent, 62–63; imagist techniques in, 48–51; opening of, 12; optimism of, 52–53; naturalism in, 36–37; as Nietzschean tragedy, 54–56; oral poetry and, 64–66; original title for, 48; as parable, 27–28, 47–48, 54; paragraph pattern in, 50; practical Christianity in, 46–48; prose rhythm in, 27; Pulitzer Prize won by, 10; as realistic fiction, 62–63; structure of, 35, 43–45; style of, 5, 11, 24, 25–27, 48–51, 64–66; symbolism in, 41–43; as tall tale, 27; unoriginality of, 24–26; verbal repetition in, 5, 45, 64–66; voyage motif in, 45, 62; women in, 56–58

PRIDE, as theme, 13, 20, 31, 32, 39, 60

SANTIAGO: as Christ-like, 14, 19, 20, 27, 28–30, 34–35, 39, 42, 46, 67–68; as Dionysian, 54–56; earlier Hemingway heroes and, 45, 58; eros and, 40–41; faith of, 30, 38–40, 46–47; as having gone out too far, 20, 32, 33, 54, 61; Hemingway's relation to, 5–6, 13–14, 28, 51–53, 63; lightheadedness of, 17–19; new knowledge gained by, 29–30, 33, 39–41; Nick Adams compared to, 45; as pathetic figure, 35–38, 49; and his role in the novel, 12–23; Saint James and, 59–60; solitude of, 15, 32, 38–40, 42, 45, 49; Spanish background of, 58–60; as tragic hero, 30–35; and village, 22, 43; youthful arm-wrestling match of, 16, 34

SEA: as Dionysian, 55; as eternal, 53; as feminine, 14, 31, 33, 39, 55, 62; multiple meanings of, 44–45; and its role in the novel, 7, 22–23, 41

SHARKS: as literary critics, 5–6, 19, 63; and their role in the novel, 19–21, 32, 39, 41–42, 44, 47, 53

SUCCESS, as theme, 35–38, 53

SUFFERING, as theme, 17, 28–30, 34–35

TEMPEST, THE (Shakespeare), and how it compares, 52

TO HAVE AND HAVE NOT, and how it compares, 23, 31, 40

TOURISTS, and their role in the novel, 21, 33, 44, 57–58

UNITY, as theme, 33, 55–56

WHITMAN, WALT, Hemingway compared to, 7